JEREM

Anglican classics in the Fyfield series

Richard Hooker
Ecclesiastical Polity: Selections

William Law
Selected Writings

Jeremy Taylor
Selected Writings

JEREMY TAYLOR

Selected Writings

*edited with an introduction
by C.H. Sisson*

FyfieldBooks

First published in Great Britain 1990 by
Carcanet Press Limited
208-212 Corn Exchange Buildings
Manchester M4 3BQ

Selection and introduction
copyright © 1990 C.H. Sisson

British Library Cataloguing in Publication Data
Taylor, Jeremy *1613-1667*
　Selected writings.
　1. Church of England. Sermons
　I. Title
　252.03

ISBN 0-85635-861-4

The publisher acknowledges financial assistance
from the Arts Council of Great Britain

Typeset in 10pt Palatino by Bryan Williamson, Darwen
Printed and bound in England by SRP Ltd, Exeter

Contents

Introduction		7
Editorial Note		15

I The Golden Grove (1655)
    To the pious and devout reader   17

II The Great Exemplar (1649)
    1 The imitation of the life of Christ   21
    2 The Nativity   33
    3 The Resurrection   36

III Holy Living (1650)
    1 Care of our time   42
    2 Purity of intention   50
    3 The practice of the presence of God   58
    4 Sobriety   67
    5 Chastity: rules for married persons   71
    6 Contentedness   74
    7 Rules and measures of justice in bargaining   84
    8 Faith   87

IV Holy Dying (1651)
    1 The vanity and shortness of man's life   93
    2 The miseries of man's life   99
    3 Exercising charity during our whole life   104
    4 A dying man's sorrow and danger   107
    5 Sickness   110
    6 Impatience   113
    7 A peroration   115

V Sermons (1651-3)
    1 A funeral sermon   116
    2 The righteous cause oppressed   127

VI The Liberty of Prophesying (1647)
    1 Heresy   130
    2 Toleration   130

Introduction

'No one need be excessively puzzled by Taylor.' That was the judgement of a man who knew all Taylor's voluminous works as well, probably, as anyone in the twentieth century. C.J. Stranks was no remote theologian, with all the academic facilities at his disposal, but a missionary in Japan who took one or other volume with him on 'nearly all the long journeys and frequent waits at way-side stations' which his life there entailed. The point is worth making at the beginning of this small selection from the works in question. No one coming fresh to the author should be intimidated by his reputation as one of the most learned divines of an age when learning was not always so lightly worn.

Jeremy Taylor was born in Cambridge in 1613 or, to stick more closely to what is precisely known, he was baptized there on 15 August of that year. He was the fourth child of Nathaniel Taylor, a barber, and his wife Mary. Some, anxious to promote the family socially, have tried to make out that Nathaniel was at least a barber-surgeon, but this appears to be without foundation. His son's real piece of luck was to have been born in a university town in which Dr Stephen Perse, a Fellow of Caius College, had left money, on his death in 1615, for the founding of a free school. The first pupils were admitted to the Perse School in 1619, when Jeremy was six years old, and it was to the Perse School that he went. The pupils' day lasted from six in the morning to five in the afternoon, with only a break of two hours. The menu of instruction was hardly what a child would encounter nowadays: the elements of the Christian religion, Latin, rhetoric. From the Perse School Jeremy entered Gonville and Caius College in 1626, the year after Charles I, with whose fate his own career was to be so involved, came to the throne. He graduated in 1630/31, and in 1633 he was awarded a junior Fellowship, like his original bursary one on the Perse foundation. People grew up earlier in those days, and it is thought that he may have been ordained before he was twenty-one.

It was chance – unless one chooses to say, unfashionably, that it was divine Providence – which caused him to be summoned to preach in London, at St Paul's, in place of an older Caius colleague. He did so well that Archbishop Laud heard of him, and invited – or perhaps ordered – him to preach at Lambeth. This may be said to have determined the whole course of Taylor's career thereafter. He vacated his fellowship at Caius and moved to Oxford, apparently with Laud's backing, and after some slight hitches was appointed to a Fellowship of All Souls. Shortly afterwards he was appointed chaplain to Charles I and in 1638 he became rector of Uppingham. These were not quiet times for the clergy of the Church of England. In 1642, when the Civil War had begun, Taylor joined the king in Oxford. He served as a chaplain in the Royalist army, and after what was to be the first of three imprisonments under the Commonwealth he retired to Wales, where he became Chaplain to the Earl of Carbery at Golden Grove in Carmarthenshire. This was a time when loyal and orthodox clergy were ejected from their livings, and Taylor was lucky to have found such a refuge. It was at Golden Grove that he wrote much of his best work. In 1658, after a period in London, he went to Lisburn in Northern Ireland, which led, after the Restoration in 1660, to his being appointed Bishop of Down and Connor and Vice-Chancellor of Dublin University. It was in Ireland, amidst many troubles personal and public, that he died in 1667.

In introducing Taylor to new readers of the late twentieth century, one has to ask why they may be tempted to explore this author's works. His will probably not be one of the names which comes first to mind, if they were asked who were the greatest prose writers in the English language. Yet Coleridge reckoned Jeremy Taylor with Shakespeare, Bacon and Milton, and found his works 'a perpetual feast'. The tastes and prejudices of our age have told against the tastes and prejudices of centuries in which explicitly Christian writers were more prominent. Moreover, our fashions have been against the sort of verbal splendours with which Taylor's works are embellished. There are good grounds for being suspicious of rhetoric, in sermons as well as in advertising matter, but it needs only a slight acquaintance with

Taylor to understand that there is no insincerity here. Read like a novel or a poem, the strangeness of his most glowing passages reveals a literary master who is compelled to use the language he does to bring the reader close to the inmost thoughts of a mind which is not only gentle and luminous but humane and generous. The reader will quickly discover, too, that if there are pages which strike first by their verbal beauty, there are others which impress above all by their simplicity and practicality. The object throughout is to establish the truth about the intimate workings of the human mind and essential psychological – he would say, spiritual – needs.

Although a theologian of great learning, Taylor was far from being a man who sought to entangle his listeners and readers with fine and debatable points. Such points occasionally pop up, as they do in all the divines of his time, for they then had a current importance, but his persistent concern is to remove hindrances to agreement among Christians, and to present what he thought were the essentials of the Faith. He says of Christ: 'He entered the world with all the circumstances of poverty... We must follow him that was crowned with thorns and sorrows... that deserved all good and suffered all evil: that is the sum of the Christian religion as it distinguishes from all the religions of the world.' If we now hear more about what the religions of the world have in common, and about what people should *not* be expected to suffer, that does not invalidate Taylor's summary. The modern reader is not entitled to dismiss it because the perspectives of our own day are different. The religious battles of his day were bitter enough, and he was himself deeply involved in the violence and suffering they caused.

The central dispute in the England of his time, complicated of course as such things always are by political differences and by economic and financial troubles whose bearing was imperfectly understood – as is still the case with our own troubles, whatever claims we may make to greater sophistication in such matters – was between the historical Church of England whose essential point of view was defined, so far as may be, in the Prayer Book, and the multifarious groups of Puritans and Independents who preferred their own ideas. The history is long and complicated, but what must be understood, if one is at all to understand Taylor's orientation, is that the Church's cause was broadly identified with that of the king and the less traditional groups with what passed for being that of Parliament, which however was destroyed by Cromwell when it became too tiresome. In 1645 the Prayer Book was made illegal and was replaced by a *Directory of Public Worship*, which indicated roughly what should be said but left ministers who valued their ingenuity to inflict on their congregations whatever expressions of piety they thought best in the inspiration of the moment. Bishops were abolished and stubborn parish priests were ejected; there were revolutionary committees in every county to ensure that only politically acceptable persons could have their say in church. The Church of England, as a public presence, ceased to exist, and it was a ministry re-constituted from scattered remnants which, after the Restoration, adopted the only slightly revised Prayer Book of 1662.

Taylor's first years as a priest fell in the period when the Puritan party was gathering strength for its ultimate seizure of power in Church and State, and his early works reflect the issues then being debated. His first published work was *A Sermon Preached upon the Anniversary of the Gunpowder Treason* – it was the anniversary of Guy Fawkes's attempt, in 1605, to blow up James I in his parliament. Taylor perhaps felt the need to dissociate himself publicly from the Roman Catholics the more strongly because he had, at Oxford, been a friend of the Franciscan theologian Christopher Davenport. This sermon was published in 1638, and was followed by *Of the Sacred Order and Offices of the Episcopacy* (1642) and *A Discourse concerning Prayer* (1646), both works dealing with matters in which he took a different view from the Puritans.

Yet although his whole career shows that he was never afraid to speak out, at whatever disadvantage to himself, the work of his most productive period shows him as concerned with those matters on which all Christians should be able to agree, and which had a bearing on the holy living and holy dying of ordinary non-theological Christians. *The Liberty of Prophesying* (1647) was described by Sir James Fitzjames Stephen, writing 250 years after it was written, as a statement of the grounds of 'the doctrine of general toleration – a doctrine which had a very long road to travel' after Taylor's day, 'before its truth was generally and fully recognised.' Taylor, it is true, 'assumes that there are some things which it is a positive duty to believe...' According to him, if a man rejected an article of the Creed from pride,

> he would be a heretic, but if he rejected it because in good faith he thought it would be false, he would not... He goes with such minuteness into the question whether the doctrines of adult baptism and transsubstantiation may be tolerated, and concludes that they may be, inasmuch as they are capable of being held in good faith, and neither can be shown to be in any respect injurious to the public.

This analysis by a man like Stephen, a leading rationalist in his time, shows how close Taylor was to what has become a prominent strand in the thinking of our own time, and went further than any apologist for any other Church went in the seventeenth century. In one respect, however, the *Liberty of Prophesying* showed an immovability which not only astonished Stephen but would be widely controverted in the twentieth century. Taylor would not extend toleration to those who thought they were too holy to submit to civil government. 'Religion is to meliorate the condition of a people,' he said, 'not to do it a disadvantage; and, therefore, those doctrines that inconvenience the public are no parts of true religion.' At the back of this is the thought that, in a remote Roman province, Christ submitted to the government of the Emperor Tiberius. It does bear thinking about.

In 1649, on 30 January of which Charles I was beheaded, it is thought by the common hangman who had earlier torn the Prayer Book to pieces and burned it, *The Great Exemplar* was published. The 'exemplar' was not Charles; the book is a life of Christ, the first ever to be written in English. It is a huge work, of more than half a million words, and there is no question of its having been written for a political occasion. It was a work designed to promote the common Christianity which was so threatened by the troubles of the time. It consists of sections of narrative, followed by discourses and prayers. 'My great purpose', Taylor says in his Preface, 'is to advance the necessity, and to declare the manner and parts of a good life'. It is concerned with that 'which will never be obtained by disputing', and so belongs, like *Holy Living* and *Holy Dying*, to the eirenic core of Taylor's work.

The Rule and Exercises of Holy Living – to give the book its full title – appeared shortly afterwards, in 1650. It is the most accessible of Taylor's works and was much in the hands of churchpeople for generations; it is profitable reading now not only for practising Christians but for anyone free enough from contemporary prejudices to want to know what the intimate meaning of Christianity was for people before the progressive secularization of our society had got properly under way. No student of our older literature can afford to ignore it, for without some understanding of these matters there can be no proper appreciation of what was in the mind of older writers who, if differently educated, were assuredly no more stupid than those of our own day. The popular notion of Christianity, in the late twentieth century, is certainly so inadequate and, one might say, degraded, that it provides no entrée to the serious writing of the past, without some knowledge of which our reading even of contemporary work will be defective. *Holy Living* is divided into four chapters, each of three to ten sections – a structure which makes the book easy for the curious to sample. The first section of the first chapter deals with 'care of our time, and the manner of spending it', which might certainly suggest that most of the many hours now spent watching television are somewhat misapplied. The second section deals with 'Purity of Intention or Purpose in all our Actions', which is a psychological as well as a moral study. The second chapter gets down to more specific matters – temperance, chastity, humility, modesty and contentedness. The third chapter begins with a section on the unpopular subject of obedience, and goes on to the justice superiors owe to their inferiors, the negotiation of contracts, and restitution where it is to be made. The final chapter alone deals with the subject 'Of Christian Religion', as more commonly understood, and only the final section of it with 'Preparation to, and the manner how to receive, the Sacrament of the Lord's Supper.'

The Rule and Exercises of Holy Dying came next, in 1651. The arrangement follows that of the companion volume, and if the matter is less likely to appeal to readers at large in an age which thinks only of avoiding death or of reaching it in good physical shape, it contains some of the author's most eloquent prose. Moreover, if most people are now less familiar with death than in the days when so many died at a relatively early age and in a domestic milieu, it still comes to us all, and the problems of sickness and of caring for the sick are still with us. So the element of practicality is here, if less ubiquitously than in *Holy Living*. Taylor was married and had children; his first wife died, and after an interval he married again, so neither book carries any suggestion of being the work of a priest without domestic responsibilities of his own. It is perhaps not irrelevant to the tone of these books that, if Taylor was relatively fortunate as compared with some in the hard times he lived in, he came from what then counted as humble origins and his career was certainly such that he must have had his share of ordinary financial worries. John Keble, writing to J.T. Coleridge in 1817, says: 'I never read *Holy Living and Dying* till this spring, and I cannot tell you the delight it has given me; surely that book is enough to convert an infidel, so gentle in heart, and so high in mind, so fervent in zeal, and so charitable in judgement...'

Although the newcomer to Taylor might, in general, do well not to start with the sermons – unless, perhaps, he already has some acquaintance with the older literature of that kind – they are for the most part extremely readable, at once lucid and rich in images. If the sentences are often long, they break up easily enough and there is nothing abstruse or tiresome about them. For all the light and sparkle with which Taylor decorates his oratory, the bricks he builds it with are homely phrases. *Twenty-five Sermons* were published in 1653; the others came later. Other later works include *Unum Necessarium, or The Doctrine and Practice of Repentance* (1655), *The Worthy Communicant* and *Ductor Dubitantium* (1660), the last-named a huge volume on cases of conscience, a subject in which Taylor had long been interested, naturally perhaps for a theologian to whom the response to religion was so important.

There is one small work, popular in its day, which deserves mention in conclusion. This is *The Golden Grove* (1655). It is a practical guide to devotion, containing 'what is to be believed, practised and desired or prayed for', and includes a simple series of questions and answers no doubt intended to serve as a substitute for the Catechism in the banned Book of Common Prayer. By this time Cromwell had dismissed Parliament and ruled with only the help of the army and, in the matter of religion, the Independents were in the ascendancy. Taylor's perspective is wider than that, and the interest of this little book is by no means merely historical. 'In this sad declension of religion,' Taylor begins '... the supplanters are gone out, and are digging down the foundations.' He speaks of these people as having 'discountenanced an excellent liturgy, taken off the hinges of unity,' and 'disgraced the articles of religion.' Readers of this address to the Reader may think some of it not irrelevant to our own times.

Editorial Note

In the arrangement of these extracts, the editor has made some departures from the chronological order of the works. He has set first – as the best possible preface to the selection as a whole – the address 'To the pious and devout reader' which Taylor designed for his little manual entitled *The Golden Grove* (1655). The extracts from *The Liberty of Prophesying* (1647) have been relegated to the end of the volume, not because they are unimportant in themselves, but because their subject-matter will be better understood by a reader who already has some acquaintance with Taylor's wider approach to the Christian faith.

The text is taken from Taylor's *Collected Works* in 10 volumes (1847-54), edited by R. Heber and C.P. Eden; this is a revision of Heber's original collected edition in 15 volumes (1822).

The volume by C.J. Stranks mentioned at the beginning of the introduction is his *Life and Writings of Jeremy Taylor* (1952).

I

The Golden Grove

TO THE PIOUS AND DEVOUT READER

In this sad declension of religion, the seers who are appointed to be the watchmen of the church, cannot but observe that the supplanters and underminers are gone out, and are digging down the foundations: and having destroyed all public forms of ecclesiastical government, discountenanced an excellent liturgy, taken off the hinges of unity, disgraced the articles of religion, polluted public assemblies, taken away all cognisance of schism, by mingling all sects, and giving countenance to that against which all power ought to stand upon their guard, there is now nothing left but that we take care that men be Christians: for concerning the ornament and advantages of religion, we cannot make that provision we desire; *Incertis de salute, de gloria minime certandum.* For since they who have seen Jerusalem in prosperity, and have forgotten the order of the morning and evening sacrifice, and the beauty of the temple, will be tempted to neglect so excellent a ministration, and their assembling themselves together for peace and holy offices, and be content with any thing that is brought to them, though it be but the husks and acorns of prodigals and swine, so they may enjoy their lands and their money with it; we must now take care that the young men who were born in the captivity, may be taught how to worship the God of Israel after the manner of their forefathers, till it shall please God that religion shall return into the land, and dwell safely, and grow prosperously.

But never did the excellency of episcopal government appear so demonstratively and conspicuously as now. Under their conduct and order we had a church so united, so orderly, so governed, a religion so settled, articles so true, sufficient, and confessed, canons so prudent and so obeyed, devotions so regular and constant, sacraments so adorned and ministered, churches so beauteous and religious, circumstances of religion so grave and prudent, so useful and apt for edification, that the enemies of our church, who serve the pope in all things, and Jesus Christ in some, who dare transgress an institution and ordinance of Christ, but dare not break a canon of the Pope, did despair of prevailing against us and truth, and knew no hopes but by setting their faces against us to destroy this government, and then they knew they should triumph without any enemy. So Balaam the son of Bosor was sent for, to curse the people of the Lord, in hope that the son of Zippor might prevail against them that long prospered under the conduct of Moses and Aaron.

But now instead of this excellency of condition and constitution of religion, the people are fallen under the harrows and saws of impertinent and ignorant preachers, who think all religion is a sermon, and all sermons ought to be libels against truth and old governors, and expound chapters that the meaning may never be understood, and pray, that they may be thought able to talk, but not to hold their peace, they casting not to obtain any thing but wealth and victory, power and plunder. And the people have reaped the fruits apt to grow upon such crabstocks: they grow idle and false, hypocrites and careless, they deny themselves nothing that is pleasant, they despise religion, forget government; and some never think of heaven; and they that do, think to go thither in such paths which all the ages of the Church did give men warning of, lest they should that way go to the devil.

But when men have tried all that they can, it is to be supposed they will return to the excellency and advantages of the christian religion, as it is taught by the Church of England; for by destroying it, no end can be served but of sin and folly, faction, and death eternal. For besides that no church that is enemy to this, does worship God in that truth of propositions, in that unblamable and pious liturgy, and in preaching the necessities of holy life, so much as the Church of England does; besides this (I say) it cannot be persecuted by any governor that understands his own interest, unless he be first abused by false preachers, and then prefers his secret opinion before his public advantage. For no church in the world is so great a friend to loyalty and obedience, as she and her sisters of the same persuasion. They that hate bishops have destroyed monarchy, and they that would erect an ecclesiastical monarchy, must consequently subject the temporal to it. And both one and the other would be supreme in consciences; and they that govern there, with an opinion that in all things they ought to be attended to, will let their prince govern others, so long as he will be ruled by them. And certainly, for a prince to persecute the protestant religion, is as if a physician should endeavour to destroy all medicaments, and fathers kill their sons, and the master of ceremonies destroy all formalities and courtships; and as if the Pope should root out all the ecclesiastic state. Nothing so combines with government, if it be of God's appointment, as the religion of the Church of England, because nothing does more adhere to the word of God, and disregard the crafty advantages of the world. If any man shall not decline to try his title by the word of God, it is certain there is not in the world a better guard for it, than the true protestant religion, as it is taught in our church. But let things be as it please God; it is certain that in that day when truth gets her victory, in that day we shall prevail against all God's enemies and ours, not in the purchases and perquisites of the world, but in the rewards and returns of holiness and patience, and faith and charity; for by these we worship God, and against this interest we cannot serve any thing else.

In the meantime we must by all means secure the foundation, and take care that religion may be conveyed in all its material parts, the same as it was, but by new and permitted instruments. For let us secure that our young men be good Christians, it is easy to make them good protestants, unless they be abused with prejudice, and suck venom with their milk; they cannot leave our communion till they have reason to reprove our doctrine.

There is therefore in the following pages a compendium of what we are to believe, – what to do, – and what to desire; it is indeed very little, but it is enough to begin with, and will serve all persons so long as they need milk, and not strong meat. And he that hath given the following assistances to thee, desires to be even a door-keeper in God's house, and to be a servant of the meanest of God's servants, and thinks it a worthy employment to teach the most ignorant, and make them to know Christ, though but in the first rudiments of a holy institution. This only he affirms, that there is more solid comfort and material support to a Christian spirit in one article of faith, in one period of the Lord's prayer, in one holy lesson, than in all the disputes of impertinent people, who take more pains to prove there is a purgatory, than to persuade men to avoid hell: and that a plain catechism can more instruct a soul, than the whole day's prate which some daily spit forth, to bid men 'get Christ,' and persecute His servants.

Christian religion is admirable for its wisdom, for its simplicity; and he that presents the following papers to thee, designs to teach thee as the Church was taught in the early days of the apostles; – to believe that Christian faith, and to understand it; to represent plain rules of good life; to describe easy forms of prayer; to bring into your assemblies hymns of glorification and thanksgiving, and psalms of prayer. By these easy paths they lead Christ's little ones into the fold of their great bishop; and if by this any service be done to God, any ministry to the soul of a child or an ignorant woman, it is hoped that God will accept it: and it is reward enough, if by my ministry God will bring it to pass that any soul shall be instructed, and brought into that state of good things that it shall rejoice for ever.

But do thou pray for him that desires this to thee, and endeavours it,

JER. TAYLOR

II

The Great Exemplar

1 AN EXHORTATION TO THE IMITATION OF THE LIFE OF CHRIST

However the person of Jesus Christ was depressed with a load of humble accidents, and shadowed with the darknesses of poverty and sad contingencies, so that the Jews, and the contemporary ages of the Gentiles, and the apostles themselves, could not at first discern the brightest sense of divinity; yet as a beauty, artificially covered with a thin cloud of cypress, transmits its excellency to the eye, made more greedy and apprehensive by that imperfect and weak restraint; so was the sanctity and holiness of the life of Jesus glorious in its darknesses, and found confessors and admirers even in the midst of those despites which were done Him upon the contrariant designs of malice and contradictory ambition. Thus the wife of Pilate called Him, "that just person"; Pilate pronounced Him "guiltless"; Judas said He was "innocent"; the devil himself called Him "the Holy one of God". For however it might concern any man's mistaken ends, to mislike the purpose of His preaching and spiritual kingdom, and those doctrines which were destructive of their complacencies and carnal securities; yet they could not deny but that He was a man of God, of exemplar sanctity, of an angelical chastity, of a life sweet, affable, and complying with human conversation, and as obedient to government as the most humble children of the kingdom, and yet He was Lord of all the world.

2. And certainly very much of this was with a design that He might shine to all the generations and ages of the world, and become a guiding star and a pillar of fire to us in our journey. For we, who believe that Jesus was perfect God and perfect man, do also believe, that one minute of His intolerable passion, and every action of His, might have been satisfactory, and enough for the expiation and reconcilement of ten thousand worlds; and

God might, upon a less effusion of blood, and a shorter life of merit, if He had pleased, have accepted human nature to pardon and favour: but, that the holy Jesus hath added so many excellent instances of holiness, and so many degrees of passion, and so many kinds of virtues, is, that He might become an example to us, and reconcile our wills to Him, as well as our persons to His heavenly Father.

3. And indeed it will prove but a sad consideration, that one drop of blood might be enough to obtain our pardon, and the treasures of His blood running out till the fountain itself was dry, shall not be enough to procure our conformity to Him; that the smallest minute of His expense shall be enough to justify us, and the whole magazine shall not procure our sanctification; that at a smaller expense God might pardon us, and at a greater we will not imitate Him: for therefore "Christ hath suffered for us", saith the apostle, "leaving an example to us, that we might follow His steps". [1 Peter ii. 21] The least of our wills cost Christ as much as the greatest of our sins. And therefore He calls Himself "the way, the truth, and the life"; that as He redeems our souls from death to life, by becoming life to our persons; so He is the truth to our understandings, and the way to our will and affections, enlightening that, and leading these in the paths of a happy eternity.

4. When the king of Moab was pressed hard by the sons of Isaac [2 Kings iii. 27], the Israelites and Edomites, he took the king of Edom's eldest son, or, as some think, his own son, the heir of his kingdom, and offered him as a holocaust upon the wall; and the Edomites presently raised the siege at Kir-haraseth, and went to their own country. The same, and much more, was God's design, who took not His enemy's, but His own son, His only-begotten Son, and God Himself, and offered Him up in sacrifice, to make us leave our perpetual fightings against heaven; and if we still persist, we are hardened beyond the wildnesses of the Arabs and Edomites, and neither are receptive of the impresses of pity nor humanity, who neither have compassion to the suffering of Jesus Christ, nor compliance with the designs of God, nor conformity to the holiness and obedience of our guide. In a dark night, if an *ignis fatuus* do but precede us, the

glaring of its lesser flames does so amuse our eyes that we follow it into rivers and precipices, as if the ray of that false light were designed on purpose to be our path to tread in: and therefore not to follow the glories of the Sun of righteousness, who indeed leads us over rocks and difficult places, but secures us against the danger and guides us into safety, is both the greatest indecency and unthankfulness in the world.

5. In the great counsel of eternity, when God set down the laws and knit fast the eternal bands of predestination, He made it one of His great purposes to make His Son like us, that we also might be like His holy Son; He, by taking our nature; we, by imitating His holiness: "God hath predestinated us to be conformable to the image of His Son", saith the apostle [Romans viii. 29]. For the first in every kind is in nature propounded as the pattern of the rest; and as the sun, the prince of all the bodies of light, and the fire of all warm substances, is the principal, the rule and the copy, which they in their proportions imitate and transcribe; so is the Word incarnate the great example of all the predestinate; for "He is the first-born among many brethren" [Romans viii. 29]. And therefore it was a precept of the apostle, and by his doctrine we understand its meaning, "put ye on the Lord Jesus Christ" [Romans xiii. 14]: the similitude declares the duty: as a garment is composed and made of the same fashion with the body, and is applied to each part in its true figure and commensuration; so should we put on Christ, and imitate the whole body of His sanctity, conforming to every integral part, and express Him in our lives, that God, seeing our impresses, may know whose image and superscription we bear, and we may be acknowledged for sons, when we have the air, and features, and resemblances of our elder brother.

6. In the practice of this duty we may be helped by certain considerations, which are like the proportion of so many rewards. For this, according to the nature of all holy exercises, stays not for pay till its work be quite finished, but (like music in churches) is pleasure, and piety, and salary besides: so is every work of grace; full of pleasure in the execution, and is abundantly rewarded, besides the stipend of a glorious eternity.

7. First: I consider that nothing is more honourable than to be like God; and the heathens, worshippers of false deities, grew vicious upon that stock; and we who have fondnesses of imitation, counting a deformity full of honour, if by it we may be like our prince, (for pleasures were in their height in Capreæ because Tiberius there wallowed in them, and a wry neck in Nero's court was the mode of gallantry,) might do well to make our imitations prudent and glorious; and, by propounding excellent examples, heighten our faculties to the capacities of an evenness with the best of precedents. He that strives to imitate another, admires Him, and confesses his own imperfections; and therefore, that our admirations be not flattering, nor our confessions fantastic and impertinent, it were but reasonable to admire Him, from whom really all perfections do derive, and before whose glories all our imperfections must confess their shame and needs of reformation. God, by a voice from heaven, and by sixteen generations of miracles and grace, hath attested the holy Jesus to be the fountain of sanctity, and the "wonderful counsellor", and "the captain of our sufferings", and the guide of our manners, by being His beloved Son, in whom He took pleasure and complacency to the height of satisfaction: and if any thing in the world be motive of our affections or satisfactory to our understandings, what is there in heaven or earth we can desire or imagine beyond a likeness to God, and participation of the divine nature and perfections? And therefore as, when the sun arises, every man goes to his work, and warms himself with his heat, and is refreshed with his influences, and measures his labour with his course; so should we frame all the actions of our life by His light who hath shined by an excellent righteousness, that we no more walk in darkness, or sleep in lethargies, or run a gazing after the lesser and imperfect beauties of the night. It is the weakness of the organ that makes us hold our hand between the sun and us, and yet stand staring upon a meteor or an inflamed jelly. And our judgments are as mistaken, and our appetites are as sottish, if we propound to ourselves, in the courses and designs of perfections, any copy but of Him, or something like Him, who is the most perfect. And lest we think His glories too great to behold,

8. Secondly: I consider, that the imitation of the life of Jesus is a duty of that excellency and perfection, that we are helped in it, not only by the assistance of a good and a great example, which possibly might be too great, and scare our endeavours and attempts; but also by its easiness, compliance, and proportion to us. For Jesus, in His whole life, conversed with men with a modest virtue, which, like a well kindled fire fitted with just materials, casts a constant heat; not like an inflamed heap of stubble, glaring with great emissions, and suddenly stooping into the thickness of smoke. His piety was even, constant, unblamable, complying with civil society, without affrightment of precedent, or prodigious instances of actions greater than the imitation of men. For if we observe our blessed Saviour in the whole story of His life, although He was without sin, yet the instances of His piety were the actions of a very holy, but of an ordinary life: and we may observe this difference in the story of Jesus from ecclesiastical writings of certain beatified persons, whose life is told rather to amaze us and to create scruples, than to lead us in the evenness and serenity of a holy conscience. Such are the prodigious penances of Simeon Stylites, the abstinence of the religious retired into the mountain Nitria, but especially the stories of later saints, in the midst of a declining piety and aged Christendom, where persons are represented holy by way of idea and fancy, if not to promote the interests of a family and institution. But our blessed Saviour, though His eternal union and adherencies of love and obedience to His heavenly Father were next to infinite, yet in His external actions, in which only, with the correspondence of the Spirit in those actions, He propounds Himself imitable, He did so converse with men, that men, after that example, might for ever converse with Him. We find that some saints have had excrescencies and eruptions of holiness in the instances of uncommanded duties, which in the same particulars we find not in the story of the life of Jesus. John Baptist was a greater mortifier than his Lord was, and some princes have given more money than all Christ's family did whilst He was alive; but the difference which is observable is, that although some men did some acts of counsel in order to attain

that perfection which in Jesus was essential and unalterable, and was not acquired by degrees and means of danger and difficulty, yet no man ever did his whole duty save only the holy Jesus. The best of men did sometimes actions not precisely and strictly requisite, and such as were besides the precept; but yet in the greatest flames of their shining piety they prevaricated something of the commandment. They that have done the most things beyond, have also done some things short of their duty; but Jesus, who intended Himself the example of piety, did in manners as in the rule of faith, which, because it was propounded to all men, was fitted to every understanding; it was true, necessary, short, easy, and intelligible: so was His rule and His copy fitted, not only with excellencies worthy, but with compliances possible to be imitated; of glories so great, that the most early and constant industry must confess its own imperfections; and yet so sweet and humane, that the greatest infirmity, if pious, shall find comfort and encouragement. Thus God gave His children *manna* from heaven; and though it was excellent, like the food of angels, yet it conformed to every palate, according to that appetite which their several fancies and constitutions did produce.

9. But now, when the example of Jesus is so excellent that it allures and tempts with its facility and sweetness, and that we are not commanded to imitate a life whose story tells of ecstacies in prayer, and abstractions of senses, and immaterial transportations, and fastings to the exinanition of spirits, and disabling all animal operations; but a life of justice and temperance, of chastity and piety, of charity and devotion; such a life, without which human society cannot be conserved, and by which, as our irregularities are made regular, so our weaknesses are not upbraided, nor our miseries made a mockery: we find so much reason to address ourselves to a heavenly imitation of so blessed a pattern, that the reasonableness of the thing will be a great argument to chide every degree and minute of neglect. It was a strange and a confident encouragement, which Phocion used to a timorous Greek, who was condemned to die with him, "is it not enough to thee that thou must die with Phocion?" I am sure, he that is most incurious of the issues of his life, is yet willing

enough to reign with Jesus, when he looks upon the glories represented without the duty; but it is a very great stupidity and unreasonableness, not to live with Him in the imitation of so holy and so prompt a piety. It is glorious to do what He did, and a shame to decline His sufferings, when there was a God to hallow and sanctify the actions, and a man clothed with infirmity to undergo the sharpness of the passion; so that the glory of the person added excellency to the first, and the tenderness of the person excused not from suffering the latter.

10. Thirdly: Every action of the life of Jesus, as it is imitable by us, is of so excellent merit, that by making up the treasure of grace, it becomes full of assistances to us, and obtains of God grace to enable us to its imitation, by way of influence and impetration. For as in the acquisition of habits, the very exercise of the action does produce a facility to the action, and in some proportion becomes the cause of itself; so does every exercise of the life of Christ kindle its own fires, inspires breath into itself, and makes an univocal production of itself in a different subject. And Jesus becomes the fountain of spiritual life to us, as the prophet Elisha to the dead child; when he stretched his hands upon the child's hands, laid his mouth to his mouth, and formed his posture to the boy, and breathed into him, the spirit returned again into the child at the prayer of Elisha; so when our lives are formed into the imitation of the life of the holiest Jesus, the Spirit of God returns into us, not only by the efficacy of the imitation, but by the merit and impetration of the actions of Jesus. It is reported in the Bohemian story, that St. Wenceslaus their king one winter night going to his devotions in a remote church, barefooted in the snow and sharpness of unequal and pointed ice, his servant Podavivus, who waited upon his master's piety, and endeavoured to imitate his affections, began to faint through the violence of the snow and cold, till the king commanded him to follow him, and set his feet in the same footsteps which his feet should mark for him: the servant did so, and either fancied a cure, or found one; for he followed his prince, helped forward with shame and zeal to his imitation, and by the forming footsteps for him in the snow. In the same manner does the blessed Jesus; for, since our

way is troublesome, obscure, full of objection and danger, apt to be mistaken and to affright our industry, He commands us to mark His footsteps, to tread where His feet have stood, and not only invites us forward by the argument of His example, but He hath trodden down much of the difficulty, and made the way easier and fit for our feet. For He knows our infirmities, and Himself hath felt their experience – in all things but in the neighbourhoods of sin; and therefore He hath proportioned a way and a path to our strengths and capacities, and like Jacob, hath marched softly and in evenness with the children and the cattle, to entertain us by the comforts of His company, and the influences of a perpetual guide.

11. Fourthly: But we must know, that not every thing which Christ did, is imitable by us; neither did He, in the work of our redemption, in all things imitate His heavenly Father. For there are some things which are issues of an absolute power, some are expresses of supreme dominion, some are actions of a judge. And therefore Jesus prayed for His enemies, and wept over Jerusalem, when at the same instant His eternal Father laughed them to scorn; for He knew that their day was coming, and Himself had decreed their ruin. But it became the holy Jesus to imitate His Father's mercies; for Himself was the great instrument of the eternal compassion, and was the instance of mercy; and therefore, in the operation of His Father's design, every action of His was univocal, and He shewed the power of His divinity in nothing but in miracles of mercy, and illustrations of faith, by creating arguments of credibility. In the same proportion we follow Jesus, as Himself followed His Father: for what He abated by the order to His intendment and design, we abate by the proportions of our nature; for some excellent acts of His were demonstrations of divinity, and an excellent grace poured forth upon Him without measure was their instrument; to which proportions if we should extend our infirmities, we should crack our sinews, and dissolve the silver cords, before we could entertain the instances and support the burden. Jesus fasted forty days and forty nights; but the manner of our fastings hath been in all ages limited to the term of an artificial day, and in the primitive

observations and the Jewish rites men did eat their meal as soon as the stars shone in the firmament. We never read that Jesus laughed, and but once that He rejoiced in spirit; but the declensions of our natures cannot bear the weight of a perpetual grave deportment, without the intervals of refreshment and free alacrity. Our ever blessed Saviour suffered the devotion of Mary Magdalene to transport her to an expensive expression of her religion, and twice to anoint His feet with costly nard; and yet if persons whose conditions were of no greater lustre or resplendency of fortune than was conspicuous in His family and retinue, should suffer the same profusion upon the dressing and perfuming their bodies, possibly it might be truly said, "it might better be sold and distributed to the poor". This Jesus received, as He was the Christ and anointed of the Lord; and by this He suffered Himself to be designed to burial, and He received the oblation as eucharistical for the ejection of seven devils; for "therefore she loved much".

12. The instances are not many. For however Jesus had some extraordinary transvolations and acts of emigration beyond the lines of His even and ordinary conversation, yet it was but seldom; for His being exemplary was of so great consideration, that He chose to have fewer instances of wonder that He might transmit the more of an imitable virtue. And therefore we may establish this for a rule and limit of our imitations; because Christ, our lawgiver, hath described all His Father's will in sanctions and signature of laws; whatsoever He commanded, and whatsoever He did, of precise morality, or in pursuance of the laws of nature, in that we are to trace His footsteps; and in these His laws and His practice differ but as a map and a guide, a law and a judge, a rule and a precedent. But in the special instances of action, we are to abate the circumstances, and to separate the obedience from the effect: whatsoever was moral in a ceremonial performance, that is highly imitable; and the obedience of sacrificing, and the subordination to laws actually in being, even now they are abrogated, teach us our duty, in a differing subject, upon the like reason. Jesus's going up to Jerusalem to the feasts, and His observation of the sabbaths, teach us our duty in celebration of

festivals constituted by a competent and just authority: for that which gave excellency to the observation of Mosaical rites, was an evangelical duty; and the piety of obedience did not only consecrate the observations of Levi, but taught us our duty in the constitutions of Christianity.

13. Fifthly: As the holy Jesus did some things which we are not to imitate, so we also are to do some things which we cannot learn from His example. For there are some of our duties which presuppose a state of sin, and some suppose a violent temptation and promptness to it; and the duties of prevention, and the instruments of restitution, are proper to us, but conveyed only by precept and not by precedent. Such are all the parts and actions of repentance, the duties of mortification and self-denial. For whatsoever the holy Jesus did in the matter of austerity, looked directly upon the work of our redemption, and looked back only on us by a reflex act, as Christ did on Peter, when He looked him into repentance. Some states of life also there are, which Jesus never led; such are those of temporal governors, kings and judges, merchants, lawyers, and the state of marriage: in the course of which lives many cases do occur, which need a precedent and the vivacity of an excellent example, especially since all the rules which they have have not prevented the subtilty of the many inventions which men have found out, nor made provision for all contingencies. Such persons in all their special needs are to govern their actions by the rules of proportion, by analogy to the holiness of the person of Jesus, and the sanctity of His institution; considering what might become a person professing the discipline of so holy a master, and what He would have done in the like case; taking our heights by the excellency of His innocency and charity. Only remember this, that in such cases we must always judge on the strictest side of piety and charity, if it be a matter concerning the interest of a second person; and that in all things we do those actions which are farthest removed from scandal, and such as towards ourselves are severe, towards others, full of gentleness and sweetness; for so would the righteous and merciful Jesus have done: these are the best analogies and proportions. And in such cases when the wells are dry, let us take

water from a cistern, and propound to ourselves some exemplar saint the necessities of whose life have determined his piety to the like occurrences.

14. But now from these particulars we shall best account to what the duty of the imitation of Jesus does amount: for it signifies, that we "should walk as He walked", tread in His steps, with our hand upon the guide, and our eye upon His rule; that we should do glory to Him, as He did to His Father; and that whatsoever we do, we should be careful that it do Him honour, and no reproach to His institution; and then account these to be the integral parts of our duty, which are imitation of His actions, or His spirit, of His rule, or of His life; there being no better imitation of Him than in such actions as do Him pleasure, however He hath expressed or intimated the precedent.

15. He that gives alms to the poor, takes Jesus by the hand; he that patiently endures injuries and affronts, helps Him to bear His cross; he that comforts his brother in affliction, gives an amiable kiss of peace to Jesus; he that bathes his own and his neighbour's sins in tears of penance and compassion, washes his master's feet: we lead Jesus into the recesses of our heart by holy meditations; and we enter into His heart, when we express Him in our actions: for so the apostle says, "he that is in Christ, walks as He also walked" [1 John ii. 6]. But thus the actions of our life relate to Him by way of worship and religion; but the use is admirable and effectual, when our actions refer to Him as to our copy, and we transcribe the original to the life. He that considers with what affections and lancinations of spirit, with what effusions of love, Jesus prayed, what fervours and assiduity, what innocency of wish, what modesty of posture, what subordination to His Father, and conformity to the divine pleasure, were in all His devotions, is taught and excited to holy and religious prayer; the rare sweetness of His deportment in all temptations and violences of His passion, His charity to His enemies, His sharp reprehensions to the Scribes and Pharisees, His ingenuity toward all men, are living and effectual sermons to teach us patience, and humility, and zeal, and candid simplicity, and justice in all our actions. I add no more instances, because all the following dis-

courses will be prosecutions of this intendment: and the life of Jesus is not described to be like a picture in a chamber of pleasure, only for beauty, and entertainment of the eye; but like the Egyptian hieroglyphics, whose every feature is a precept, and the images converse with men by sense, and signification of excellent discourses.

16. It was not without great reason advised, that every man should propound the example of a wise and virtuous personage, as Cato, or Socrates, or Brutus; and by a fiction of imagination to suppose him present as a witness, and really to take his life as the direction of all our actions. The best and most excellent of the old lawgivers and philosophers among the Greeks had an allay of viciousness, and could not be exemplary all over: some were noted for flatterers, as Plato and Aristippus; some for incontinency, as Aristotle, Epicurus, Zeno, Theognis, Plato, and Aristippus again; and Socrates, whom their oracle affirmed to be the wisest and most perfect man, yet was by Porphyry noted for extreme intemperance of anger, both in words and actions: and those Romans who were offered to them for examples, although they were great in reputation, yet they had also great vices; Brutus dipped his hand in the blood of Cæsar, his prince, and his father by love, endearments, and adoption; and Cato was but a wise man all day, at night he was used to drink too liberally; and both he and Socrates did give their wives unto their friends; the philosopher and the censor were procurers of their wives' unchastity: and yet these were the best among the Gentiles. But how happy and richly furnished are Christians with precedents of saints, whose faith and revelations have been productive of more spiritual graces and greater degrees of moral perfections! And this I call the privilege of a very great assistance, that I might advance the reputation and account of the life of the glorious Jesu, which is not abated by the imperfections of human nature, as they were, but receives great heightenings and perfection from the divinity of His person, of which they were never capable.

17. Let us therefore press after Jesus, as Elisha did after his master, with an inseparable prosecution, even whithersoever He goes; that, according to the reasonableness and proportion

expressed in St. Paul's advice, "as we have borne the image of the earthly, we may also bear the image of the heavenly" [1 Cor. xv. 49]; for "in vain are we called Christians, if we live not according to the example and discipline of Christ, the father of the institution". When St. Laurence was in the midst of the torments of the gridiron, he made this to be the matter of his joy and eucharist, that he was admitted to the gates through which Jesus had entered; and therefore thrice happy are they who walk in His courts all their days: and it is yet a nearer union and vicinity to imprint His life in our souls, and express it in our exterior converse; and this is done by him only, who (as St. Prosper describes that duty) despises all those gilded vanities which He despised, that fears none of those sadnesses which He suffered, that practises or also teaches those doctrines which He taught, and hopes for the accomplishment of all His promises. And this is truest religion, and the most solemn adoration.

2 THE NATIVITY OF OUR BLESSED SAVIOUR JESUS

1. The holy maid longed to be a glad mother; and she who carried a burden whose proper commensuration is the days of eternity, counted the tedious minutes, expecting when the Sun of righteousness should break forth from His bed, where nine months He hid Himself as behind a fruitful cloud. About the same time, God, who in His infinite wisdom does concentre and tie together in one end things of disparate and disproportionate natures, making things improbable to co-operate to what wonder or to what truth He pleases, brought the holy Virgin to Bethlehem, the city of David, "to be taxed" with her husband Joseph, according to a decree upon all the world, issuing from Augustus Cæsar. But this happened in this conjunction of time, that it might be fulfilled which was spoken by the prophet Micah, "and thou Bethlehem in the land of Judah art not the least among the princes of Judah, for out of thee shall come a governor that shall rule My people Israel". This rare act of providence was highly remarkable,

because this taxing seems wholly to have been ordered by God to serve and minister to the circumstances of this birth. For this taxing was not in order to tribute: Herod was now king, and received all the revenues of the *fiscus*, and paid to Augustus an appointed tribute, after the manner of other kings, friends and relatives of the Roman empire; neither doth it appear that the Romans laid a new tribute on the Jews before the confiscation of the goods of Archelaus. Augustus therefore, sending special delegates to tax every city, made only an inquest after the strength of the Roman empire in men and monies; and did himself no other advantage, but was directed by Him who rules and turns the hearts of princes, that he might, by verifying a prophecy, signify and publish the divinity of the mission and the birth of Jesus.

2. She that had conceived by the operation of that Spirit who dwells within the element of love, was no ways impeded in her journey by the greatness of her burden; but arrived at Bethlehem in the throng of strangers, who had so filled up the places of hospitality and public entertainment, that "there was no room" for Joseph and Mary "in the inn". But yet she felt that it was necessary to retire where she might softly lay her burden, who began now to call at the gates of His prison, and nature was ready to let Him forth. But she that was mother to the king of all the creatures, could find no other but a stable, a cave of a rock, whither she retired; where, when it began to be with her after the manner of women, she humbly bowed her knees, in the posture and guise of worshippers, and in the midst of glorious thoughts and highest speculations "brought forth her first-born into the world".

3. As there was no sin in the conception, so neither had she pains in the production, as the church, from the days of Gregory Nazianzen until now, hath piously believed; though before his days there were some opinions to the contrary, but certainly neither so pious, nor so reasonable. For to her alone did not the punishment of Eve extend, that "in sorrow she should bring forth": for where nothing of sin was an ingredient, there misery cannot cohabit. For though amongst the daughters of men many

conceptions are innocent and holy, being sanctified by the word of God and prayer, hallowed by marriage, designed by prudence, seasoned by temperance, conducted by religion towards a just, a hallowed, and a holy end, and yet their productions are in sorrow; yet this of the blessed Virgin might be otherwise, because here sin was no relative, and neither was in the principle nor the derivative, in the act nor in the habit, in the root nor in the branch: there was nothing in this but the sanctification of a virgin's womb, and that could not be the parent of sorrow, especially that gate not having been opened by which the curse always entered. And as to conceive by the Holy Ghost was glorious, so to bring forth any of "the fruits of the Spirit" is joyful, and full of felicities. And He that came from His grave fast tied with a stone and signature, and into the college of apostles "the doors being shut", and into the glories of His Father through the solid orbs of all the firmament, came also (as the Church piously believes) into the world so without doing violence to the virginal and pure body of His mother, that He did also leave her virginity entire, to be as a seal, that none might open the gate of that sanctuary; that it might be fulfilled which was spoken of the Lord by the prophet, "This gate shall be shut, it shall not be opened, and no man shall enter in by it; because the Lord God of Israel hath entered by it, therefore it shall be shut" [Ezekiel xliv. 2].

4. Although all the world were concerned in the birth of this great Prince, yet I find no story of any one that ministered at it, save only angels, who knew their duty to their Lord, and the great interests of that person; whom, as soon as He was born, they presented to His mother, who could not but receive Him with a joy next to the rejoicings of glory and beatific vision, seeing Him to be born her son, who was the Son of God, of greater beauty than the sun, purer than angels, more loving than the seraphims, as dear as the eye and heart of God, where He was from eternity engraven, His beloved and His only-begotten.

5. When the virgin mother now felt the first tenderness and yearnings of a mother's bowels, and saw the Saviour of the world born, poor as her fortunes could represent Him, naked as the innocence of Adam, she took Him, and "wrapt Him in swaddling-

clothes"; and after she had a while cradled Him in her arms, she "laid Him in a manger"; for so was the design of His humility; that as the last scene of His life was represented among thieves, so the first was amongst beasts, the sheep and the oxen; according to that mysterious hymn of the prophet Habakkuk, "His brightness was as the light; He had horns coming out of His hand, and there was the hiding of His power" [Hab. iii. 4].

6. But this place, which was one of the great instances of His humility, grew to be as venerable as became an instrument; and it was consecrated into a church, the crib into an altar, where first lay that "Lamb of God", which afterwards was sacrificed for the sins of all the world. And when Adrian the emperor, who intended a great despite to it, built a temple to Venus and Adonis in that place where the holy virgin-mother, and her more holy Son, were humbly laid; even so he could not obtain but that even amongst the gentile inhabitants of the neighbouring countries it was held in an account far above scandal and contempt. For God can ennoble even the meanest of creatures, especially if it be but a relative and instrumental to religion, higher than the injuries of scoffers and malicious persons. But it was then a temple full of religion, full of glory, when angels were the ministers, the holy Virgin was the worshipper, and Christ the deity.

3   OF THE RESURRECTION AND ASCENSION OF JESUS

1. While it was yet "early in the morning, upon the first day of the week, Mary Magdalen, and Mary the mother of James, and Salome, brought sweet spices to the sepulchre", that they might again embalm the holy body (for the rites of embalming among the Hebrews used to last forty days), and their love was not satisfied with what Joseph had done. They therefore hastened to the grave; and after they had expended their money and bought the spices, then begin to consider "who shall remove the stone": but yet they still go on, and their love answers the objection, not knowing how it should be done, but yet resolving

to go through all the difficulties; but never remember or take care to pass the guards of soldiers. But when they came to the sepulchre, they found the guard affrighted and removed, and the stone rolled away; for there had a little before their arrival been a great earthquake; and an angel descending from heaven, rolled away the stone, and sat upon it; and for fear of him the guards about the tomb became astonished with fear, and were like dead men: and some of them ran to the high priests, and told them what happened. But they, now resolving to make their iniquity safe and unquestionable, by a new crime hire the soldiers to tell an incredible and a weak fable, that His disciples came by night and stole Him away, against which accident the wit of man could give no more security than themselves had made. The women entered into the sepulchre, and missing the body of Jesus, Mary Magdalen ran to the eleven apostles, complaining that the body of our Lord was not to be found. Then Peter and John ran as fast as they could to see: for the unexpectedness of the relation, the wonder of the story, and the sadness of the person, moved some affections in them, which were kindled by the first principles and sparks of faith, but were not made actual and definite, because the faith was not raised to a flame: they looked into the sepulchre, and finding not the body there, they returned. By this time Mary Magdalen was come back; and the women who staid weeping for their Lord's body, saw two angels sitting in white, the one at the head, and the other at the feet: at which unexpected sight they trembled, and bowed themselves: but an angel bid them not to fear, telling them that Jesus of Nazareth, who was crucified, was also risen, and was not there: and called to mind what Jesus had told them in Galilee concerning His crucifixion, and resurrection the third day.

2. And Mary Magdalen turned herself back, and saw Jesus; but supposing Him to be the gardener, she said to Him, "Sir, if thou have borne Him hence, tell me where thou hast laid Him, and I will take Him away". But Jesus said unto her, "Mary!" Then she knew His voice, and with ecstasy of joy and wonder was ready to have crushed His feet with her embraces: but He commanded her not to touch Him, but to go to His brethren, and say,

"I ascend unto My Father and to your Father, to My God and your God". Mary departed with satisfaction, beyond the joys of a victory or a full vintage, and told these things to the apostles; but the narration seemed to them as talk of abused and fantastic persons. – About the same time Jesus also appeared unto Simon Peter. – Towards the declining of the day, two of His disciples going to Emmaus, sad, and discoursing of the late occurrences, Jesus puts Himself into their company, and upbraids their incredulity; and expounds the scriptures, that Christ ought to suffer, and rise again the third day; and in the breaking of bread disappeared, and so was known to them by vanishing away, whom present they knew not: and instantly they hasten to Jerusalem, and told the apostles what had happened.

3. And while they were there, that is, the same day at evening, when the apostles were assembled, all save Thomas, secretly, for fear of the Jews, the doors being shut, Jesus came and stood in the midst of them. They were exceedingly troubled, supposing it had been a spirit. But Jesus confuted them by the philosophy of their senses, by feeling His flesh and bones, which spirits have not. For He gave them His benediction, shewing them His hands and His feet. At which sight they rejoiced with exceeding joy, and began to be restored to their indefinite hopes of some future felicity by the return of their Lord to life: and there He first breathed on them, giving them the holy Ghost, and performing the promise twice made before His death; the promise of the keys, or of binding and loosing, saying, "whosoever sins ye remit, they are remitted to them: and whosoever sins ye retain, they are retained": and that was the second part of clerical power with which Jesus instructed His disciples, in order to their great commission of preaching and government ecclesiastical. These things were told to Thomas, but he believed not, and resolved against the belief of it, unless He might put his finger into His hands, and his hand into His side. Jesus therefore on the octaves of His resurrection appeared again to the apostles met together, and makes demonstration to Thomas; in conviction and reproof of his unbelief promising a special benediction to all succeeding ages of the Church; for they are such who "saw not, and yet have believed".

4. But Jesus at His early appearing had sent an order by the women, that the disciples should go into Galilee; and they did so after a few days. And Simon Peter being there, went a fishing, and six other of the apostles with him, to the sea of Tiberias; where they laboured all night and caught nothing. Towards the morning, Jesus appeared to them, and bade them cast the net on the right side of the ship; which they did, and enclosed an hundred and fifty-three great fishes: by which prodigious draught John, the beloved disciple, perceived it was the Lord. At which instant, Peter threw himself into the sea, and went to Jesus; and when the rest were come to shore, they dined with broiled fish. After dinner Jesus, taking care for those scattered sheep which were dispersed over the face of the earth, that He might gather them into one sheepfold under one Shepherd, asked Peter, "Simon, son of Jonas, lovest thou Me more than these? Peter answered, Yea, Lord; Thou, that knowest all things, knowest that I love Thee; then Jesus said unto him, Feed My lambs". And Jesus asked him the same question, and gave him the same precept the second time, and the third time: for it was a considerable and a weighty employment, upon which Jesus was willing to spend all His endearments and stock of affections that Peter owed Him, even upon the care of His little flock. And after the intrusting of this charge to him, He told him that the reward he should have in this world, would be a sharp and an honourable martyrdom; and withal checks at Peter's curiosity, in busying himself about the temporal accidents of other men, and enquiring what should become of John, the beloved disciple. Jesus answered his question with some sharpness of reprehension, and no satisfaction: "If I will that he tarry till I come, what is that to thee?" Then they fancied that he should not die; but they were mistaken, for the intimation was expounded and verified by St. John's surviving the destruction of Jerusalem; for after the attempts of persecutors, and the miraculous escape of prepared torments, he died a natural death in a good old age.

5. After this Jesus, having appointed a solemn meeting for all the brethren that could be collected from the dispersion, and named a certain mountain in Galilee, appeared to five hundred

brethren at once; and this was His most public and solemn manifestation; and while some doubted, Jesus came according to his designation, and spake to the eleven; sent them to preach to all the world repentance, and remission of sins in His name; promising to be with them to the end of the world. – He appeared also unto James, but at what time is uncertain, save that there is something concerning it in the gospel of St. Matthew which the Nazarenes of Berœa used; and which it is likely themselves added out of report, for there is nothing of it in our Greek copies. The words are these: "When the Lord had given the linen in which He was wrapped to the servant of the high priest, He went and appeared unto James; for James had vowed after he received the Lord's supper, that he would eat no bread till he saw the Lord risen from the grave: then the Lord called for bread: He blessed it, and brake it, and gave it to James the just, and said, 'My brother, eat bread, for the Son of man is risen from the sleep of death'": so that by this it should seem to be done upon the day of the resurrection; but the relation of it by St. Paul puts it between the appearance which He made to the five hundred, and that last to the apostles when He was to ascend into heaven. – Last of all, when the apostles were at dinner, He appeared to them, upbraiding their incredulity; and then He opened their understanding that they might discern the sense of scripture, and again commanded them to preach the gospel to all the world, giving them power to do miracles, to cast out devils, to cure diseases; and instituted the sacrament of baptism, which He commanded should, together with the sermons of the gospel, be administered to all nations, In the name of the Father, and of the Son, and of the holy Ghost. Then He led them into Judea, and they came to Bethany, and from thence to the mount Olivet; and He commanded them to stay in Jerusalem, till the holy Ghost, the promise of the Father, should descend upon them, which should be accomplished in a few days; and then they should know the times, and the seasons, and all things necessary for their ministration and service, and propagation of the gospel. And while He discoursed many things concerning the kingdom, behold a cloud came and parted Jesus from them, and carried Him in their sight up into heaven; where He sits at the right hand of God, blessed for ever. Amen.

6. While His apostles stood gazing up to heaven, two angels appeared to them, and told them that Jesus should come in like manner as He was taken away, viz. with glory and majesty, and in the clouds, and with the ministry of angels.

"Amen. Come, Lord Jesus; come quickly".

III

Holy Living

CARE OF OUR TIME

He that is choice of his time will also be choice of his company, and choice of his actions: lest the first engage him in vanity and loss; and the latter, by being criminal, be a throwing his time and himself away, and a going back in the accounts of eternity.

God hath given to man a short time here upon earth, and yet upon this short time eternity depends; but so that for every hour of our life, after we are persons capable of laws and know good from evil, we must give account to the great Judge of men and angels. And this is it which our blessed Saviour told us, that we must account for every idle word: not meaning that every word which is not designed to edification, or is less prudent, shall be reckoned for a sin; but that the time which we spend in our idle talking and unprofitable discoursings, that time which might and ought to have been employed to spiritual and useful purposes, that is to be accounted for.

For we must remember that we have a great work to do, many enemies to conquer, many evils to prevent, much danger to run through, many difficulties to be mastered, many necessities to serve, and much good to do, many children to provide for, or many friends to support, or many poor to relieve, or many diseases to cure, besides the needs of nature and of relation, our private and our public cares, and duties of the world which necessity and the providence of God hath adopted into the family of religion.

And that we need not fear this instrument to be a snare to us, or that the duty must end in scruple, vexation, and eternal fears, we must remember that the life of every man may be so ordered, and indeed must, that it be a perpetual serving of God: the greatest trouble and most busy trade and worldly incumbrances, when they are necessary, or charitable, or profitable in order to any of those ends which we are bound to serve, whether public or private, being a doing God's work. For God provides the good things of the world to serve the needs of nature by the labours of the ploughman, the skill and pains of the artisan, and the dangers and traffic of the merchant: these men are in their calling the ministers of the divine providence, and the stewards of the creation, and servants of a great family of God, the world, in the employment of procuring necessaries for food and clothing, ornament and physic. In their proportions also a king and a priest and a prophet, a judge and an advocate, doing the works of their employment according to their proper rules, are doing the work of God, because they serve those necessities, which God hath made, and yet made no provisions for them but by their ministry. So that no man can complain that his calling takes him off from religion: his calling itself and his very worldly employment in honest trades and offices is a serving of God; and if it be moderately pursued, and according to the rules of Christian prudence, will leave void spaces enough for prayers and retirements of a more spiritual religion.

God hath given every man work enough to do, that there shall be no room for idleness; and yet hath so ordered the world that there shall be space for devotion: he that hath the fewest businesses of the world, is called upon to spend more time in the dressing of his soul; and he that hath the most affairs, may so order them that they shall be a service of God; whilst at certain periods they are blessed with prayers and actions of religion, and all day long are hallowed by a holy intention.

However, so long as idleness is quite shut out from our lives, all the sins of wantonness, softness, and effeminacy, are prevented, and there is but little room left for temptation; and therefore to a busy man temptation is fain to climb up together with his businesses, and sins creep upon him only by accidents and occasions: whereas to an idle person they come in a full body, and with open violence, and the impudence of a restless importunity.

Idleness is called the sin of Sodom and her daughters [Ezekiel xvi. 49], and indeed is 'the burial of a living man'; an idle person being so useless to any purposes of God and man that he is like one that is dead, unconcerned in the changes and necessities of the world; and he only lives to spend his time, and eat the fruits of the earth: like a vermin or a wolf; when their time comes they die and perish, and in the mean time do no good; they neither plough nor carry burdens; all that they do either is unprofitable or mischievous.

Idleness is the greatest prodigality in the world: it throws away that which is invaluable in respect of its present use, and irreparable when it is past, being to be recovered by no power of art or nature.

But the way to secure and improve our time we may practise in the following rules.

Rules for employing our time

1. In the morning when you awake, accustom yourself to think first upon God, or something in order to His service; and at night also let Him close thine eyes: and let your sleep be necessary and healthful, not idle and expensive of time, beyond the needs and conveniences of nature; and sometimes be curious to see the preparation which the sun makes when he is coming forth from his chambers of the east.

2. Let every man that hath a calling be diligent in pursuance of its employment, so as not lightly or without reasonable occasion to neglect it in any of those times which are usually, and by the custom of prudent persons and good husbands, employed in it.

3. Let all intervals or void spaces of time be employed in prayers, reading, meditating, works of nature, recreation, charity, friendliness and neighbourhood, and means of spiritual and corporal health: ever remembering so to work in our calling as not to neglect the work of our high calling; but to begin and end the day with God, with such forms of devotion as shall be proper to our necessities.

4. The resting days of Christians, and festivals of the church, must in no sense be days of idleness; for it is better to plough

upon holy days, than to do nothing or to do viciously: but let them be spent in the works of the day, that is, of religion and charity, according to the rules appointed.

5. Avoid the company of drunkards and busy bodies, and all such as are apt to talk much to little purpose: for no man can be provident of his time, that is not prudent in the choice of his company; and if one of the speakers be vain, tedious, and trifling, he that hears, and he that answers, in the discourse, are equal losers of their time.

6. Never walk with any man, or undertake any trifling employment, merely to pass the time away: for every day well spent may become a 'day of salvation', and time rightly employed is an 'acceptable time'. And remember that the time thou triflest away was given thee to repent in, to pray for pardon of sins, to work out thy salvation, to do the work of grace, to lay up against the day of judgment a treasure of good works, that thy time may be crowned with eternity.

7. In the midst of the works of thy calling, often retire to God in short prayers and ejaculations; and those may make up the want of those larger portions of time, which, it may be, thou desirest for devotion, and in which thou thinkest other persons have advantage of thee; for so thou reconcilest the outward work and thy inward calling, the church and the commonwealth, the employment of the body and the interest of thy soul: for be sure that God is present at thy breathings and hearty sighings of prayer, as soon as at the longer offices of less busied persons; and thy time is as truly sanctified by a trade, and devout though shorter prayers, as by the longer offices of those whose time is not filled up with labour and useful business.

8. Let your employment be such as may become a reasonable person; and not be a business fit for children or distracted people, but fit for your age and understanding. For a man may be very idly busy, and take great pains to so little purpose, that in his labours and expense of time he shall serve no end but of folly and vanity. There are some trades that wholly serve the ends of idle persons and fools, and as such are fit to be seized upon by the severity of laws and banished from under the sun; and there

are some people who are busy, but it is as Domitian was, in catching flies.

9. Let your employment be fitted to your person and calling. Some there are that employ their time in affairs infinitely below the dignity of their person; and being called by God, or by the republic, to help bear great burdens, and to judge a people, do enfeeble their understandings, and disable their persons by sordid and brutish business. Thus Nero went up and down Greece, and challenged the fiddlers at their trade. Aeropus, a Macedonian king, made lanterns. Harcatius, the king of Parthia, was a molecatcher: and Biantes, the Lydian, filed needles. He that is appointed to minister in holy things, must not suffer secular affairs and sordid arts to eat up great portions of his employment: a clergyman must not keep a tavern, nor a judge be an innkeeper; and it was a great idleness in Theophylact, the patriarch of C.P. to spend his time in his stable of horses, when he should have been in his study, or the pulpit, or saying his holy offices. Such employments are the diseases of labour, and the rust of time, which it contracts, not by lying still, but by dirty employment.

10. Let our employment be such as becomes a Christian; that is, in no sense, mingled with sin: for he that takes pains to serve the ends of covetousness, or ministers to another's lust, or keeps a shop of impurities or intemperance, is idle in the worst sense; for every hour or so spent runs him backward, and must be spent again in the remaining and shorter part of his life, and spent better.

11. Persons of great quality, and of no trade, are to be most prudent and curious in their employment and traffic of time. They are miserable if their education hath been so loose and undisciplined as to leave them unfurnished of skill to spend their time; but most miserable are they, if such misgovernment and unskilfulness make them fall into vicious and baser company, and drive on their time by the sad minutes and periods of sin and death. They that are learned know the worth of time, and the manner how well to improve a day; and they are to prepare themselves for such purposes in which they may be most useful in order to arts or arms, to counsel in public, or government in

their country: but for others of them that are unlearned, let them choose good company, such as may not tempt them to a vice, or join with them in any; but that may supply their defects by counsel and discourse, by way of conduct and conversation. Let them learn easy and useful things, read history and the laws of the land, learn the customs of their country, the condition of their own estate, profitable and charitable contrivances of it: let them study prudently to govern their families, learn the burdens of their tenants, the necessities of their neighbours, and in their proportion supply them, and reconcile their enmities, and prevent their law-suits, or quickly end them; and in this glut of leisure and disemployment, let them set apart greater portions of their time for religion and the necessities of their souls.

12. Let the women of noble birth and great fortunes do the same thing in their proportions and capacities, nurse their children, look to the affairs of the house, visit poor cottages, and relieve their necessities, be courteous to the neighbourhood, learn in silence of their husbands or their spiritual guides, read good books, pray often and speak little, and "learn to do good works for necessary uses"; for by that phrase St. Paul expresses the obligation of christian women to good housewifery and charitable provisions for their family and neighbourhood.

13. Let all persons of all conditions avoid all delicacy and niceness in their clothing or diet, because such softness engages them upon great misspendings of their time, while they dress and comb out all their opportunities of their morning devotion, and half the day's severity, and sleep out the care and provision for their souls.

14. Let every one of every condition avoid curiosity, and all enquiry into things that concern them not. For all business in things that concern us not is an employing our time to no good of ours, and therefore not in order to a happy eternity. In this account our neighbour's necessities are not to be reckoned; for they concern us, as one member is concerned in the grief of another; but going from house to house, tattlers and busy bodies, which are the canker and rust of idleness, as idleness is the rust of time, are reproved by the apostle in severe language, and forbidden in order to this exercise.

15. As much as may be, cut off all impertinent and useless employments of your life, unnecessary and fantastic visits, long waitings upon great personages, where neither duty, nor necessity, nor charity obliges us; all vain meetings, all laborious trifles, and whatsoever spends much time to no real civil, religious, or charitable purpose.

16. Let not your recreations be lavish spenders of your time; but choose such which are healthful, short, transient, recreative, and apt to refresh you; but at no hand dwell upon them, or make them your great employment: for he that spends his time in sports, and calls it recreation, is like him whose garment is all made of fringes, and his meat nothing but sauces; they are healthless, chargeable, and useless. And therefore avoid such games which require much time or long attendance; or which are apt to steal thy affections from more severe employments. For to whatsoever thou hast given thy affections, thou wilt not grudge to give thy time. Natural necessity and the example of St. John, who recreated himself with sporting with a tame partridge, teach us that it is lawful to relax and unbend our bow, but not to suffer it to be unready or unstrung.

17. Set apart some portions of every day for more solemn devotion and religious employment, which be severe in observing: and if variety of employment, or prudent affairs, or civil society press upon you, yet so order thy rule that the necessary parts of it be not omitted; and though just occasions may make our prayers shorter, yet let nothing but a violent, sudden, and impatient necessity, make thee upon any one day wholly to omit thy morning and evening devotions; which if you be forced to make very short, you may supply and lengthen with ejaculations and short retirements in the day time, in the midst of your employment or of your company.

18. Do not the "work of God negligently" [Jer. xlviii. 10] and idly: let not thy heart be upon the world, when thy hand is lift up in prayer: and be sure to prefer an action of religion, in its place and proper season, before all worldly pleasure, letting secular things, that may be dispensed with in themselves, in these circumstances wait upon the other: not like the patriarch, who

ran from the altar in St. Sophia to his stable, in all his pontificals, and in the midst of his office, to see a colt newly fallen from his beloved and much valued mare Phorbante. More prudent and severe was that of Sir Thomas More, who, being sent for by the king when he was at his prayers in public, returned answer, he would attend him, when he had first performed his service to the King of kings. And it did honour to Rusticus that when letters from Cæsar were given to him, he refused to open them till the philosopher had done his lecture. In honouring God and doing His work, put forth all thy strength; for of that time only thou mayest be most confident that it is gained, which is prudently and zealously spent in God's service.

19. When the clock strikes, or however else you shall measure the day, it is good to say a short ejaculation every hour, that the parts and returns of devotions may be the measure of your time: and do so also in all the branches of thy sleep; that those spaces, which have in them no direct business of the world, may be filled with religion.

20. If by thus doing you have not secured your time by an early and fore-handed care, yet be sure by a timely diligence to redeem the time, that is, to be pious and religious in such instances in which formerly you have sinned, and to bestow your time especially upon such graces the contrary whereof you have formerly practised, doing actions of chastity and temperance with as great a zeal and earnestness as you did once act your uncleanness; and then by all arts to watch against your present and future dangers, from day to day securing your standing: this is properly to redeem your time, that is, to buy your security of it at the rate of any labour and honest arts.

21. Let him that is most busied set apart some solemn time every year, in which, for the time quitting all worldly business, he may attend wholly to fasting and prayer, and the dressing of his soul by confessions, meditations, and attendances upon God [1 Cor. vii. 5]; that he may make up his accounts, renew his vows, make amends for his carelessness, and retire back again, from whence levity and the vanities of the world, or the opportunity of temptations, or the distraction of secular affairs, have carried him.

22. In this we shall be much assisted, and we shall find the work more easy, if before we sleep every night we examine the actions of the past day; with a particular scrutiny, if there have been any accident extraordinary, as long discourse, a feast, much business, variety of company: if nothing but common hath happened, the less examination will suffice; only let us take care that we sleep not without such a recollection of the actions of the day, as may represent any thing that is remarkable and great, either to be the matter of sorrow or thanksgiving: for other things a general care is proportionable.

23. Let all these things be done prudently and moderately, not with scruple and vexation. For these are good advantages, but the particulars are not divine commandments; and therefore are to be used as shall be found expedient to every one's condition. For provided that our duty be secured, for the degrees and for the instruments every man is permitted to himself and the conduct of such who shall be appointed to him. He is happy that can secure every hour to a sober or a pious employment: but the duty consists not scrupulously in minutes and half hours, but in greater portions of time; provided that no minute be employed in sin, and the great portions of our time be spent in sober employment, and all the appointed days, and some portions of every day, be allowed for religion. In all the lesser parts of time, we are left to our own elections and prudent management, and to the consideration of the great degrees and differences of glory that are laid up in heaven for us according to the degrees of our care, and piety, and diligence.

2 PURITY OF INTENTION

That we should intend and design God's glory in every action we do, whether it be natural or chosen, is expressed by St. Paul, "whether ye eat or drink, do all to the glory of God" [1 Cor. x. 31]. Which rule when we observe, every action of nature becomes religious, and every meal is an act of worship and shall have its reward in its proportion, as well as an act of prayer. Blessed be that goodness and grace of God which, out of infinite desire to glorify and save mankind, would make the very works of nature capable of becoming acts of virtue, that all our life-time we may do Him service.

This grace is so excellent that it sanctifies the most common action of our life; and yet so necessary, that without it the very best actions of our devotions are imperfect and vicious. For he that prays out of custom, or gives alms for praise, or fasts to be accounted religious, is but a Pharisee in his devotion, and a beggar in his alms, and a hypocrite in his fast. But a holy end sanctifies all these and all other actions which can be made holy, and gives distinction to them, and procures acceptance.

For as to know the end distinguishes a man from a beast, so to choose a good end distinguishes him from an evil man. Hezekiah repeated his good deeds upon his sick-bed, and obtained favour of God; but the Pharisee was accounted insolent for doing the same thing: because this man did it to upbraid his brother, the other to obtain a mercy of God. Zacharias questioned with the angel about his message, and was made speechless for his incredulity; but the blessed Virgin Mary questioned too, and was blameless; for she did it to enquire after the manner of the thing, but he did not believe the thing itself: he doubted of God's power, or the truth of the messenger; but she only of her own incapacity. This was it which distinguished the mourning of David from the exclamation of Saul; the confession of Pharaoh from that of Manasses; the tears of Peter from the repentance of Judas: for the praise is not in the deed done, but in the manner of its doing. If a man visits his sick friend, and watches at his pillow for charity's sake, and because of his old affection, we approve it: but if he does it in hope of legacy, he is a vulture, and only watches for the carcase. The same things are honest and dishonest: the manner of doing them, and the end of the design, makes the separation.

Holy intention is to the actions of a man that which the soul is to the body, or form to its matter, or the root to the tree, or the sun to the world, or the fountain to a river, or the base to a pillar: for without these the body is a dead trunk, the matter is sluggish, the tree is a block, the world is darkness, the river is quickly dry, the pillar rushes into flatness and a ruin; and the action is sinful, or unprofitable and vain. The poor farmer that gave a dish of cold water to Artaxerxes was rewarded with a golden goblet; and he that gives the same to a disciple in the name of a disciple, shall have a crown: but if he gives water in despite, when the disciple needs wine or a cordial, his reward shall be, to want that water to cool his tongue.

But this duty must be reduced to rules:–

Rules for our intentions

1. In every action reflect upon the end; and in your undertaking it, consider why you do it, and what you propound to yourself for a reward, and to your action as its end.

2. Begin every action in the name of the Father, of the Son, and of the Holy Ghost: the meaning of which is, first, that we be careful that we do not the action without the permission or warrant of God: secondly, that we design it to the glory of God, if not in the direct action, yet at least in its consequence; if not in the particular, yet at least in the whole order of things and accidents: thirdly, that it may be so blessed, that what you intend for innocent and holy purposes, may not by any chance, or abuse, or misunderstanding of men, be turned into evil, or made the occasion of sin.

3. Let every action of concernment be begun with prayer, that God would not only bless the action, but sanctify your purpose; and make an oblation of the action to God: holy and well intended actions being the best oblations and presents we can make to God; and when God is entitled to them, He will the rather keep the fire upon the altar bright and shining.

4. In the prosecution of the action, renew and re-kindle your purpose by short ejaculations to these purposes: "Not unto us, O Lord, not unto us, but unto Thy name let all praise be given": and consider, "Now I am working the work of God; I am His servant, I am in a happy employment, I am doing my master's

business, I am not at my own dispose, I am using His talents, and all the gain must be His": for then be sure, as the glory is His, so the reward shall be thine. If thou bringest His goods home with increase, He will make thee ruler over cities.

5. Have a care that while the altar thus sends up a holy fume, thou dost not suffer the birds to come and carry away the sacrifice: that is, let not that which began well, and was intended for God's glory, decline and end in thy own praise, or temporal satisfaction, or a sin. A story told to represent the vileness of unchastity, is well begun: but if thy female auditor be pleased with thy language, and begins rather to like thy person for thy story than to dislike the crime, be watchful lest this goodly head of gold descend in silver and brass, and end in iron and clay, like Nebuchadnezzar's image; for from the end it shall have its name and reward.

6. If any accidental event which was not first intended by thee, can come to pass, let it not be taken into thy purposes, nor at all be made use of: as if by telling a true story you can do an ill turn to your enemy, by no means do it; but when the temptation is found out, turn all thy enmity upon that.

7. In every more solemn action of religion, join together many good ends, that the consideration of them may entertain all your affections; and that, when any one ceases, the purity of your intention may be supported by another supply. He that fasts only to tame a rebellious body, when he is provided of a remedy either in grace or nature, may be tempted to leave off his fasting. But he that in his fast intends the mortification of every unruly appetite, and accustoming himself to bear the yoke of the Lord, a contempt of the pleasures of meat and drink, humiliation of all wilder thoughts, obedience and humility, austerity and charity, and the convenience and assistance to devotion, and to do an act of repentance, whatever happens, will have reason enough to make him to continue his purpose, and to sanctify it. And certain it is, the more good ends are designed in an action, the more degrees of excellency the man obtains.

8. If any temptation to spoil your purpose happens in a religious duty, do not presently omit the action, but rather strive to rectify

your intention, and to mortify the temptation. St. Bernard taught us this rule: for when the devil, observing him to preach excellently and to do much benefit to his hearers, tempted him to vain-glory, hoping that the good man, to avoid that, would cease preaching, he gave this answer only; "I neither began for thee, neither for thee will I make an end".

9. In all actions which are of long continuance, deliberation, and abode, let your holy and pious intention be actual; that is, that it be, by a special prayer or action, by a peculiar act of resignation or oblation, given to God: but in smaller actions, and little things and indifferent, fail not to secure a pious habitual intention; that is, that it be included within your general care, that no action have an ill end; and that it be comprehended in your general prayers, whereby you offer yourself and all you do, to God's glory.

10. Call not every temporal end a defiling of thy intention, but only, first, when it contradicts any of the ends of God; or secondly, when it is principally intended in an action of religion. For sometimes a temporal end is part of our duty; and such are all the actions of our calling, whether our employment be religious or civil. We are commanded to provide for our family: but if the minister of divine offices shall take upon him that holy calling for covetous or ambitious ends, or shall not design the glory of God principally and especially, he hath polluted his hands and his heart; and the fire of the altar is quenched, or it sends forth nothing but the smoke of mushrooms, or unpleasant gums. And it is a great unworthiness to prefer the interest of a creature before the ends of God, the almighty Creator.

But because many causes may happen in which a man's heart may deceive him, and he may not well know what is in his own spirit; therefore by these following signs we shall best make a judgment whether our intentions be pure, and our purposes holy.

Signs of purity of intention

1. It is probable our hearts are right with God, and our intentions innocent and pious, if we set upon actions of religion or

civil life with an affection proportionate to the quality of the work; that we act our temporal affairs with a desire no greater than our necessity; and that in actions of religion we be zealous, active, and operative, so far as prudence will permit; but in all cases that we value a religious design before a temporal, when otherwise they are in equal order to their several ends: that is, that whatsoever is necessary in order to our soul's health, be higher esteemed than what is for bodily; and the necessities, the indispensable necessities of the spirit, be served before the needs of nature, when they are required in their several circumstances; or plainer yet, when we choose any temporal inconvenience rather than commit a sin, and when we choose to do a duty rather than to get gain. But he that does his recreation or his merchandise cheerfully, promptly, readily, and busily, and the works of religion slowly, flatly, and without appetite, and the spirit moves like Pharaoh's chariots when the wheels were off; it is a sign that his heart is not right with God, but it cleaves too much to the world.

2. It is likely our hearts are pure, and our intentions spotless, when we are not solicitous of the opinion and censures of men; but only that we do our duty, and be accepted of God. For our eyes will certainly be fixed there from whence we expect our reward: and if we desire that God should approve us, it is a sign we do His work, and expect Him our paymaster.

3. He that does as well in private, between God and his own soul, as in public, in pulpits, in theatres, and market-places, hath given himself a good testimony that his purposes are full of honesty, nobleness, and integrity. For what Helkanah said to the mother of Samuel, "Am not I better to thee than ten sons?" is most certainly verified concerning God; that He who is to be our judge is better than ten thousand witnesses. But he that would have his virtue published, studies not virtue, but glory. "He is not just that will not be just without praise; but he is a righteous man that does justice when to do so is made infamous, and he is a wise man who is delighted with an ill name that is well gotten". And indeed that man hath a strange covetousness, or folly, that is not contented with this reward, that he hath pleased God. And see what he gets by it: he that does good works for

praise or secular ends, sells an inestimable jewel for a trifle; and that which would purchase heaven for him, he parts with for the breath of the people; which at best is but air, and that not often wholesome.

4. It is well also when we are not solicitous or troubled concerning the effect and event of all our actions; but that being first by prayer recommended to Him, is left at His dispose: for then, in case the event be not answerable to our desires or to the efficacy of the instrument, we have nothing left to rest in but the honesty of our purposes; which it is the more likely we have secured, by how much more we are indifferent concerning the success. St. James converted but eight persons, when he preached in Spain: and our blessed Saviour converted fewer than His own disciples did: and if thy labours prove unprosperous, if thou beest much troubled at that, it is certain thou didst not think thyself secure of a reward for your intention; which you might have done if it had been pure and just.

5. He loves virtue for God's sake and its own, that loves and honours it wherever it is to be seen; but he that is envious or angry at a virtue that is not his own, at the perfection or excellency of his neighbour, is not covetous of the virtue, but of its reward and reputation; and then his intentions are polluted. It was a great ingenuity in Moses that wished all the people might be prophets; but if he had designed his own honour, he would have prophesied alone. But he that desires only that the work of God and religion shall go on, is pleased with it whoever is the instrument.

6. He that despises the world and all its appendant vanities, is the best judge, and the most secured of his intentions; because he is the farthest removed from a temptation. Every degree of mortification is a testimony of the purity of our purposes; and in what degree we despise sensual pleasure, or secular honours, or worldly reputation, in the same degree we shall conclude our heart right to religion and spiritual designs.

7. When we are not solicitous concerning the instruments and means of our actions, but use those means which God hath laid before us, with resignation, indifferency, and thankfulness; it is

a good sign that we are rather intent upon the end of God's glory, than our own conveniency or temporal satisfaction. He that is indifferent whether he serve God in riches or in poverty, is rather a seeker of God than of himself; and he that will throw away a good book because it is not curiously gilded, is more curious to please his eye than to inform his understanding.

8. When a temporal end consisting with a spiritual, and pretended to be subordinate to it, happens to fail and be defeated, if we can rejoice in that, so God's glory may be secured, and the interests of religion; it is a great sign our hearts are right, and our end prudently designed and ordered.

When our intentions are thus balanced, regulated, and discerned, we may consider,

First, that this exercise is of so universal efficacy in the whole course of a holy life, that it is like the soul to every holy action, and must be provided for in every undertaking; and is of itself alone sufficient to make all natural and indifferent actions to be adopted into the family of religion.

Secondly, that there are some actions which are usually reckoned as parts of our religion, which yet of themselves are so relative and imperfect, that without the purity of intention they degenerate: and unless they be directed and proceed on to those purposes which God designed them to, they return into the family of common, secular, or sinful actions. Thus alms are for charity, fasting for temperance, prayer is for religion, humiliation is for humility, austerity or sufferance is in order to the virtue of patience: and when these actions fail of their several ends, or are not directed to their own purposes, alms are misspent, fasting is an impertinent trouble, prayer is but lip-labour, humiliation is but hypocrisy, sufferance is but vexation; for such were the alms of the Pharisee, the fast of Jezebel, the prayer of Judah reproved by the prophet Isaiah, the humiliation of Ahab, the martyrdom of heretics; in which nothing is given to God but the body, or the forms of religion; but the soul and the power of godliness is wholly wanting.

Thirdly, we are to consider that no intention can sanctify an unholy or unlawful action. Saul the king disobeyed God's commandment, and spared the cattle of Amalek to reserve the best for sacrifice: and Saul the Pharisee persecuted the Church of God, with a design to do God service: and they that killed the apostles had also good purposes, but they had unhallowed actions. When there is both truth in election, and charity in the intention; when we go to God in ways of His own choosing or approving, then our eye is single, and our hands are clean, and our hearts are pure. But when a man does evil that good may come of it, or good to an evil purpose, that man does like him that rolls himself in thorns, that he may sleep easily; he roasts himself in the fire that he may quench his thirst with his own sweat; he turns his face to the east that he may go to bed with the sun. I end this with the saying of a wise heathen: "He is to be called evil, that is good only for his own sake. Regard not how full hands you bring to God, but how pure. Many cease from sin out of fear alone, not out of innocence or love of virtue; and they as yet are not to be called innocent but timorous".

3 THE PRACTICE OF THE PRESENCE OF GOD

That God is present in all places, that He sees every action, hears all discourses, and understands every thought, is no strange thing to a Christian ear, who hath been taught this doctrine, not only by right reason, and the consent of all the wise men in the world, but also by God himself in holy scripture. "Am I a God at hand, saith the Lord, and not a God afar off? Can any hide himself in secret places, that I shall not see him? saith the Lord; do not I fill heaven and earth?" [Jer. xxiii. 23, 24]; "neither is there any creature that is not manifest in His sight, but all things are naked and open to the eyes of Him with whom we have to do" [Hebrews iv. 13]; "for in Him we live, and move, and have our being" [Acts xvii. 28]. God is wholly in every place, included in no place; not bound with cords except those of love; not divided into parts, not changeable into several shapes; filling heaven and earth with His present power, and with His never absent nature:

so St. Augustine expresses this article. So that we may imagine God to be as the air and the sea, and we all enclosed in His circle, wrapped up in the lap of His infinite nature; or as infants in the wombs of their pregnant mothers: and we can no more be removed from the presence of God than from our own being.

Several manners of the divine presence

The presence of God is understood by us in several manners, and to several purposes.

1. God is present by His essence; which, because it is infinite, cannot be contained within the limits of any place; and because He is of an essential purity and spiritual nature, He cannot be undervalued by being supposed present in the places of unnatural uncleanness: because as the sun, reflecting upon the mud of strands and shores, is unpolluted in its beams, so is God not dishonoured when we suppose Him in every of His creatures, and in every part of every one of them; and is still as unmixt with any unhandsome adherence as is the soul in the bowels of the body.

2. God is every where present by His power. He rolls the orbs of heaven with His hand; He fixes the earth with His foot; He guides all the creatures with His eye, and refreshes them with His influence: He makes the powers of hell to shake with His terrors, and binds the devils with His word, and throws them out with His command; and sends the angels on embassies with His decrees: He hardens the joints of infants, and confirms the bones, when they are fashioned beneath secretly in the earth. He it is that assists at the numerous productions of fishes; and there is not one hollowness in the bottom of the sea but He shews Himself to be Lord of it, by sustaining there the creatures that come to dwell in it: and in the wilderness, the bittern and the stork, the dragon and the satyr, the unicorn and the elk, live upon His provisions, and revere His power, and feel the force of His almightiness.

3. God is more specially present in some places by the several and more special manifestations of Himself to extraordinary

purposes. First, by glory. Thus His seat is in heaven; because there He sits encircled with all the outward demonstrations of His glory, which He is pleased to shew to all the inhabitants of those His inward and secret courts. And thus they that 'die in the Lord', may be properly said to be 'gone to God'; with whom although they were before, yet now they enter into His courts, into the secret of His tabernacle, into the retinue and splendour of His glory. That is called walking with God; but this is dwelling, or being, with Him. "I desire to be dissolved and to be with Christ"; so said St. Paul. But this manner of the divine presence is reserved for the elect people of God, and for their portion in their country.

4. God is by grace and benediction specially present in holy places [Matthew xviii. 20; Hebrews x. 25], and in the solemn assemblies of His servants. If holy people meet in grots and dens of the earth, when persecution or a public necessity disturbs the public order, circumstance and convenience, God fails not to come thither to them: but God is also, by the same or a greater reason, present there where they meet ordinarily by order, and public authority: there God is present ordinarily, that is, at every such meeting. God will go out of His way to meet His saints, when themselves are forced out of their way of order by a sad necessity: but else God's usual way is to be present in those places where His servants are appointed ordinarily to meet [1 Kings v. 9; Psalm cxxxviii. 1,2]. But His presence there signifies nothing but a readiness to hear their prayers, to bless their persons, to accept their offices, and to like even the circumstance of orderly and public meeting. For thither the prayers of consecration, the public authority separating it, and God's love of order, and the reasonable customs of religion, have, in ordinary, and in a certain degree, fixed this manner of His presence; and He loves to have it so.

5. God is especially present in the hearts of His people, by His Holy Spirit: and indeed the hearts of holy men are temples in the truth of things, and in type and shadow they are heaven itself. For God reigns in the hearts of His servants: there is His kingdom. The power of grace hath subdued all His enemies: there

is His power. They serve Him night and day, and give Him thanks and praise: that is His glory. This is the religion and worship of God in the temple. The temple itself is the heart of man; Christ is the high priest, who from thence sends up the incense of prayers, and joins them to His own intercession, and presents all together to His Father; and the Holy Ghost, by His dwelling there, hath also consecrated it into a temple [1 Cor. iii. 16; 2 Cor. vi. 16]; and God dwells in our hearts by faith, and Christ by His spirit, and the Spirit by His purities: so that we are also cabinets of the mysterious Trinity; and what is this short of heaven itself, but as infancy is short of manhood, and letters of words? The same state of life it is, but not the same age. It is heaven in a looking-glass, dark but yet true, representing the beauties of the soul, and the graces of God, and the images of His eternal glory, by the reality of a special presence.

6. God is specially present in the consciences of all persons, good and bad, by way of testimony and judgment; that is, He is there a remembrancer to call our actions to mind, a witness to bring them to judgment, and a judge to acquit or to condemn. And although this manner of presence is in this life after the manner of this life, that is, imperfect, and we forget many actions of our lives; yet the greatest changes of our state of grace or sin, our most considerable actions, are always present, like capital letters to an aged and dim eye; and at the day of judgment God shall draw aside the cloud, and manifest this manner of His presence more notoriously, and make it appear that He was an observer of our very thoughts; and that He only laid those things by, which, because we covered with dust and negligence, were not then discerned. But when we are risen from our dust and imperfection, they all appear plain and legible.

Now the consideration of this great truth is of a very universal use in the whole course of the life of a Christian. All the consequences and effects of it are universal. He that remembers that God stands a witness and a judge beholding every secrecy, besides his impiety must have put on impudence, if he be not much restrained in his temptation to sin. "For the greatest part of sin is taken away if a man have a witness of his conversation":

and he is a great despiser of God, who sends a boy away when he is going to commit fornication, and yet will dare to do it though he knows God is present, and cannot be sent off: as if the eye of a little boy were more awful than the all-seeing eye of God. He is to be feared in public, He is to be feared in private: if you go forth, He spies you; if you go in, He sees you: when you light the candle, He observes you; when you put it out, then also God marks you. Be sure that while you are in His sight, you behave yourself as becomes so holy a presence. But if you will sin, retire yourself wisely, and go where God cannot see: for no where else can you be safe. And certainly if men would always actually consider and really esteem this truth, that God is the great eye of the world, always watching over our actions, and an ever-open ear to hear all our words, and an unwearied arm ever lifted up to crush a sinner into ruin, it would be the readiest way in the world to make sin to cease from amongst the children of men, and for men to approach to the blessed estate of the saints in heaven, who cannot sin, for they always walk in the presence and behold the face of God. – This instrument is to be reduced to practice according to the following rules:–

Rules of exercising this consideration

1. Let this actual thought often return, that God is omnipresent, filling every place; and say with David, "Whither shall I go from Thy spirit, or whither shall I flee from Thy presence? If I ascend up into heaven, Thou art there: if I make my bed in hell, Thou art there", &c. [Psalm cxxxix. 7,8]. This thought by being frequent will make an habitual dread and reverence towards God, and fear, in all thy actions. For it is a great necessity and engagement to do unblameably when we act before the Judge who is infallible in His sentence, all-knowing in His information, severe in His anger, powerful in His providence, and intolerable in His wrath and indignation.

2. In the beginning of actions of religion, make an act of adoration, that is, solemnly worship God, and place thyself in God's presence, and behold Him with the eye of faith; and let thy desires

actually fix on Him as the object of thy worship, and the reason of thy hope, and the fountain of thy blessing. For when thou hast placed thyself before Him and kneelest in His presence, it is most likely all the following parts of thy devotion will be answerable to the wisdom of such an apprehension, and the glory of such a presence.

3. Let every thing you see represent to your spirit the presence, the excellency, and the power of God; and let your conversation with the creatures lead you unto the Creator; for so shall your actions be done more frequently with an actual eye to God's presence, by your often seeing Him in the glass of the creation. In the face of the sun you may see God's beauty; in the fire you may feel His heat warming; in the water, His gentleness refresh you: He it is that comforts your spirit when you have taken cordials; it is the dew of heaven that makes your field give you bread, and the breasts of God are the bottles that minister drink to your necessities. This philosophy, which is obvious to every man's experience, is a good advantage to our piety; and by this act of understanding our wills are checked from violence and misdemeanour.

4. In your retirement, make frequent colloquies or short discoursings between God and thy own soul. "Seven times a day do I prase Thee; and in the night season also I thought upon Thee while I was waking". So did David; and every act of complaint or thanksgiving, every act of rejoicing or of mourning, every petition and every return of the heart in these intercourses, is a going to God, an appearing in His presence, and a representing Him present to thy spirit and to thy necessity. And this was long since by a spiritual person called, 'a building to God a chapel in our heart'. It reconciles Martha's employment with Mary's devotion, charity and religion, the necessities of our calling and the employments of devotion. For thus in the midst of the works of your trade you may retire into your chapel, your heart; and converse with God by frequent addresses and returns.

5. Represent and offer to God acts of love and fear; which are the proper effects of this apprehension, and the proper exercise of this consideration. For as God is every where present by His

power, He calls for reverence and godly fear: as He is present to thee in all thy needs, and relieves them, He deserves thy love: and since in every accident of our lives we find one or other of these apparent, and in most things we see both, it is a proper and proportionate return that to every such demonstration of God we express ourselves sensible of it by admiring the divine goodness, or trembling at His presence; ever obeying Him because we love Him, and ever obeying Him because we fear to offend Him. This is that which Enoch did, who thus "walked with God".

6. Let us remember that God is in us, and that we are in Him: we are His workmanship, let us not deface it; we are in His presence, let us not pollute it by unholy and impure actions. God hath "also wrought all our works in us" [Isaiah xxvi. 12]; and because He rejoices in His own works, if we defile them and make them unpleasant to Him, we walk perversely with God, and He will walk crookedly towards us.

7. God is in the bowels of thy brother; refresh them when he needs it, and then you give your alms in the presence of God, and to God; and He feels the relief which thou providest for thy brother.

8. God is in every place: suppose it therefore to be a church; and that decency of deportment and piety of carriage which you are taught by religion, or by custom, or by civility and public manners, to use in churches, the same use in all places: with this difference only, that in churches let your deportment be religious in external forms and circumstances also; but there and every where, let it be religious in abstaining from spiritual undecencies, and in readiness to do good actions: that it may not be said of us, as God once complained of His people, "Why hath My beloved done wickedness in My house?" [Jer. xi. 15].

9. God is in every creature: be cruel towards none, neither abuse any by intemperance; remember that the creatures, and every member of thy own body, is one of the lesser cabinets and receptacles of God; they are such which God hath blessed with His presence, hallowed by His touch, and separated from unholy use by making them to belong to His dwelling.

10. He walks as in the presence of God that converses with Him in frequent prayer and frequent communion; that runs to Him in all his necessities, that asks counsel of Him in all his doubtings; that opens all his wants to Him; that weeps before Him for his sins; that asks remedy and support for his weakness; that fears Him as a judge, reverences Him as a lord, obeys Him as a father, and loves Him as a patron.

The benefits of this exercise

The benefits of this consideration and exercise being universal upon all the parts of piety, I shall less need to specify any particulars; but yet most properly this exercise of considering the divine presence is,

First, an excellent help to prayer, producing in us reverence and awfulness to the divine majesty of God, and actual devotion in our offices.

Secondly, it produces a confidence in God, and fearlessness of our enemies, patience in trouble, and hope of remedy; since God is so nigh in all our sad accidents; He is a disposer of the hearts of men and the events of things: He proportions out our trials, and supplies us with remedy, and, where His rod strikes us, His staff supports us. To which we may add this; that God, who is always with us, is especially by promise with us in tribulation, to turn the misery into a mercy, and that our greatest trouble may become our advantage, by entitling us to a new manner of the divine presence.

Thirdly, it is apt to produce joy and rejoicing in God, we being more apt to delight in the partners and witnesses of our conversation, every degree of mutual abiding and conversing being a relation and an endearment: we are of the same household with God; He is with us in our natural actions, to preserve us; in our recreations, to restrain us; in our public actions to applaud or reprove us; in our private, to observe us: in our sleeps, to watch by us; in our watchings, to refresh us: and if we walk with God in all His ways as He walks with us in all ours, we shall find perpetual reasons to enable us to keep that rule of God, "Rejoice in the Lord always, and again I say rejoice". And this puts me in mind of a saying of an old religious person, "There is one way of overcoming our ghostly enemies; spiritual mirth, and a perpetual bearing of God in our minds": this effectively resists the devil, and suffers us to receive no hurt from him.

Fourthly, this exercise is apt also to rekindle holy desires of the enjoyment of God, because it produces joy when we do enjoy Him; the same desires that a weak man hath for a defender, the sick man for a physician, the poor for a patron, the child for his father, the espoused lover for her betrothed.

Fifthly, from the same fountain are apt to issue humility of spirit, apprehensions of our great distance and our great needs, our daily wants and hourly supplies, admiration of God's unspeakable mercies: it is the cause of great modesty and decency in our actions; it helps to recollection of mind, and restrains the scatterings and looseness of wandering thoughts; it establishes the heart in good purposes, and leadeth on to perseverance; it gains purity and perfection, – according to the saying of God to Abraham, "walk before Me, and be perfect", – holy fear, and holy love, and indeed every thing that pertains to holy living. When we see ourselves placed in the eye of God, who sets us on work and will reward us plenteously, to serve Him with an eye-service is very pleasing, for He also sees the heart: and the want of this consideration was declared to be the cause why Israel sinned so grievously, "for they say, The Lord hath forsaken the earth, and the Lord seeth not": therefore "the land is full of blood, and the city full of perverseness" [Psalm x. 11; Ezekiel ix. 9]. What a child would do in the eye of his father, and a pupil before his tutor, and a wife in the presence of her husband, and a servant in the sight of his master, let us always do the same: for we are made a spectacle to God, to angels, and to men; we are always in the sight and presence of the all-seeing and almighty God, who also is to us a father and a guardian, a husband and a lord.

OF SOBRIETY IN THE GENERAL SENSE

Christian religion, in all its moral parts, is nothing else but the law of nature, and great reason, complying with the great necessities of all the world, and promoting the great profit of all relations, and carrying us through all accidents of variety of chances to that end which God hath from eternal ages purposed for all that live according to it, and which He hath revealed in Jesus Christ: and, according to the apostle's arithmetic, hath but these three parts of it, sobriety, justice, religion; "for the grace of God bringing salvation hath appeared to all men, teaching us that denying ungodliness and worldly lusts, we should live soberly, righteously, and godly, in this present world, looking for that blessed hope and glorious appearing of the great God and our Saviour Jesus Christ". The first contains all our deportment in our personal and private capacities, the fair treating of our bodies and our spirits; the second enlarges our duty in all relations to our neighbour; the third contains the offices of direct religion, and intercourse with God.

Christian sobriety is all that duty that concerns ourselves in the matter of meat and drink and pleasures and thoughts; and it hath within it the duties of temperance, chastity, humility, modesty, and content.

It is a using severity, denial and frustration of our appetite, when it grows unreasonable in any of these instances: the necessity of which we shall to best purpose understand, by considering the evil consequences of sensuality, effeminacy, or fondness after carnal pleasures.

Evil consequents of voluptuousness or sensuality

1. A longing after sensual pleasures is a dissolution of the spirit of a man, and makes it loose, soft, and wandering; unapt for noble, wise, or spiritual employments; because the principles upon which pleasure is chosen and pursued, are sottish, weak, and unlearned, such as prefer the body before the soul, the appetite before reason, sense before the spirit, the pleasures of a short abode before the pleasures of eternity.

2. The nature of sensual pleasure is vain, empty, and unsatisfying, biggest always in expectation, and a mere vanity in the enjoying, and leaves a sting and thorn behind it when it goes off: our laughing, if it be loud and high, commonly ends in a deep sigh; and all the instances of pleasure have a sting in the tail, though they carry beauty on the face and sweetness on the lip.

3. Sensual pleasure is a great abuse to the spirit of a man, being a kind of fascination or witchcraft, blinding the understanding and enslaving the will; and he that knows he is free-born or redeemed with the blood of the Son of God, will not easily suffer the freedom of his soul to be entangled and rifled.

4. It is most contrary to the state of a Christian, whose life is a perpetual exercise, a wrestling and warfare, to which sensual pleasure disables him, by yielding to that enemy with whom he must strive if ever he will be crowned: and this argument the apostle intimated, "he that striveth for masteries is temperate in all things; now they do it to obtain a corruptible crown, but we an incorruptible" [1 Cor. ix. 25].

5. It is by a certain consequence the greatest impediment in the world to martyrdom; that being a fondness, this being a cruelty to the flesh; to which a Christian man arriving by degrees, must first have crucified the lesser affections: for he that is overcome by little arguments of pain, will hardly consent to lose his life with torments.

Degrees of sobriety

Against this voluptuousness sobriety is opposed in three degrees.

First, a despite or disaffection to pleasures, or a resolving against all entertainment of the instances and temptations of sensuality; and it consists in the internal faculties of will and understanding decreeing and declaring against them, disapproving and disliking them, upon good reason and strong resolution.

Secondly, a fight and actual war against all the temptations and offers of sensual pleasure in all evil instances and degrees; and it consists in prayer, in fasting, in cheap diet, and hard lodging, and laborious exercises, and avoiding occasions, and using all arts and industry of fortifying the spirit, and making it severe, manly, and christian.

Thirdly, spiritual pleasure is the highest degree of sobriety; and in the same degree in which we relish and are in love with spiritual delights, the "hidden manna" [Apoc. ii. 17], with the sweetnesses of devotion, with the joys of thanksgiving, with rejoicings in the Lord, with the comforts of hope, with the deliciousness of charity and alms-deeds, with the sweetness of a good conscience, with the peace of meekness, and the felicities of a contented spirit; in the same degree we disrelish and loath the husks of swinish lusts, and the parings of the apples of Sodom; and the taste of sinful pleasures is unsavoury as the drunkard's vomit.

Rules for suppressing voluptuousness

The precepts and advices which are of best and of general use in the curing of sensuality, are these:

1. Accustom thyself to cut off all superfluity in the provisions of thy life: for our desires will enlarge beyond the present possession, so long as all the things of this world are unsatisfying; if therefore you suffer them to extend beyond the measures of necessity or moderated conveniency, they will still swell, but you reduce them to a little compass when you make nature to be your limit. We must more take care that our desires should cease, than that they should be satisfied: and therefore reducing them to narrow scantlings and small proportions is the best instrument to redeem their trouble, and prevent the dropsy, because that is next to an universal denying them; it is certainly a paring off from them all unreasonableness and irregularity: for "whatsoever covets unseemly things, and is apt to swell into an inconvenient bulk, is to be chastened and tempered: and such are sensuality, and a boy", saith the philosopher.

2. Suppress your sensual desires in their first approach; for then they are least, and thy faculties and election are stronger: but if they in their weakness prevail upon thy strengths, there

will be no resisting them when they are increased and thy abilities lessened; you shall scarce obtain of them to end, if you suffer them to begin.

3. Divert them with some laudable employment, and take off their edge by inadvertency, or a not attending to them. For since the faculties of a man cannot at the same time with any sharpness attend to two objects, if you employ your spirit upon a book or a bodily labour, or any innocent and indifferent employment, you have no room left for the present trouble of a sensual temptation. For to this sense it was that Alexander told the queen of Caria that his tutor Leonidas had provided two cooks for him, "hard marches all night, and a small dinner the next day": these tamed his youthful aptnesses to dissolution, so long as he ate of their provisions.

4. Look upon pleasures, not upon that side that is next the sun, or where they look beauteously; that is, as they come towards you to be enjoyed, for then they paint, and smile, and dress themselves up in tinsel and glass, gems and counterfeit imagery: but when thou hast rifled and discomposed them with enjoying their false beauties, and that they begin to go off, then behold them in their nakedness and weariness. See what a sigh and sorrow, what naked unhandsome proportions, and a filthy carcase, they discover; and the next time they counterfeit, remember what you have already discovered, and be no more abused. And I have known some wise persons have advised to cure the passions and longings of their children by letting them taste of every thing they passionately fancied, for they should be sure to find less in it than they looked for, and the impatience of their being denied would be loosened and made slack; and when our wishings are no bigger than the thing deserves, and our usages of them according to our needs (which may be obtained by trying what they are, and what good they can do us), we shall find in all pleasures so little entertainment, that the vanity of the possession will soon reprove the violence of the appetite. And if this permission be in innocent instances, it may be of good use: but Solomon tried it in all things, taking his fill of all pleasures, and soon grew weary of them all. The same thing we may do by reason

which we do by experience, if either we will look upon pleasures as we are sure they look when they go off, after their enjoyment: or if we will credit the experience of those men who have tasted them and loathed them.

5. Often consider and contemplate the joys of heaven, that when they have filled thy desires, which are the sails of the soul, thou mayest steer only thither, and never more look back to Sodom. And when thy soul dwells above and looks down upon the pleasures of the world, they seem like things at distance, little and contemptible, and men running after the satisfaction of their sottish appetites seem foolish as fishes, thousands of them running after a rotten worm that covers a deadly hook; or at the best but like children, with great noise pursuing a bubble rising from a walnut-shell, which ends sooner than the noise.

6. To this, the example of Christ and His apostles, of Moses, and all the wise men of all ages of the world, will much help; who, understanding how to distinguish good from evil, did choose a sad and melancholy way to felicity, rather than the broad, pleasant, and easy path, to folly and misery.

But this is but the general; its first particular is temperance.

5 RULES FOR MARRIED PERSONS, OR MATRIMONIAL CHASTITY

Concerning married persons, besides the keeping of their mutual faith and contract with each other, these particulars are useful to be observed.

1. Although their mutual endearments are safe within the protection of marriage, yet they that have wives or husbands must be as though they had them not; that is, they must have an affection greater to each other, than they have to any person in the world, but not greater than they have to God, but that they be ready to part with all interest in each other's person rather than sin against God.

2. In their permissions and licence, they must be sure to observe

the order of nature, and the ends of God. He is an ill husband that uses his wife as a man treats a harlot, having no other end but pleasure. Concerning which our best rule is, that although in this, as in eating and drinking, there is an appetite to be satisfied, which cannot be done without pleasing that desire; yet since that desire and satisfaction was intended by nature for other ends, they should never be separate from those ends, but always be joined with all or one of these ends, with a desire of children, or to avoid fornication, or to lighten and ease the cares and sadnesses of household affairs, or to endear each other; but never with a purpose, either in act or desire, to separate the sensuality from these ends which hallow it. Onan did separate his act from its proper end, and so ordered his embraces that his wife could not conceive, and God punished him.

3. Married persons must keep such modesty and decency of treating each other, that they never force themselves into high and violent lusts with arts and misbecoming devices; always remembering that those mixtures are most innocent, which are most simple and most natural, most orderly and most safe.

4. It is a duty of matrimonial chastity to be restrained and temperate in the use of their lawful pleasures: concerning which although no universal rule can antecedently be given to all persons, any more than to all bodies one proportion of meat and drink; yet married persons are to estimate the degree of their licence according to the following proportions; that it be moderate, so as to consist with health; that it be so ordered as not to be too expensive of time, that precious opportunity of working out our salvation; that when duty is demanded, it be always paid (so far as is in our powers and election) according to the foregoing measures; and that it be with a temperate affection, without violent transporting desires, or too sensual applications. Concerning which a man is to make judgment by proportion to other actions, and the severities of his religion, and the sentences of sober and wise persons: always remembering that marriage is a provision for supply of the natural necessities of the body, not for the artificial and procured appetites of the mind; and it is a sad truth that many married persons, thinking that the flood-gates of liberty are

set wide open without measures or restraints, so they sail in that channel, have felt the final rewards of intemperance and lust, by their unlawful using of lawful permissions. Only let each of them be temperate, and both of them be modest. Socrates was wont to say that those women to whom nature had not been indulgent in good features and colours, should make it up themselves with excellent manners; and those who were beautiful and comely, should be careful that so fair a body be not polluted with unhandsome usages. To which Plutarch adds, that a wife, if she be unhandsome, should consider how extremely ugly she would be, if she wanted modesty; but if she be handsome, let her think how gracious that beauty would be if she superadds chastity.

5. Married persons by consent are to abstain from their mutual entertainments at solemn times of devotion; not as a duty of itself necessary, but as being the most proper act of purity which in their condition they can present to God, and being a good advantage for attending their preparation to the solemn duty and their demeanour in it. It is St. Paul's counsel, that "by consent for a time they should abstain, that they may give themselves to fasting and prayer" [1 Cor. viii. 5]. And though when Christians did receive the holy communion every day, it is certain they did not abstain, but had children; yet when the communion was more seldom, they did with religion abstain from the marriage-bed during the time of their solemn preparatory devotions, as anciently they did from eating and drinking, till the solemnity of the day was past.

6. It were well if married persons would, in their penitential prayers, and in their general confessions, suspect themselves, and accordingly ask a general pardon for all their undecencies and more passionate applications of themselves in the offices of marriage: that what is lawful and honourable in its kind may not be sullied with imperfect circumstances, or if it be, it may be made clean again by the interruption and recallings of such a repentance of which such uncertain parts of action are capable.

But because of all the dangers of a Christian none more pressing and troublesome than the temptations to lust, no enemy more dangerous than that of the flesh, no accounts greater than what we have to reckon for at the audit of concupiscence, therefore it concerns all that would be safe from this death to arm themselves by the following rules, to prevent or to cure all the wounds of our flesh made by the poisoned arrows of lust.

6. CONTENTEDNESS

Upon the strength of these premises we may reduce this virtue to practice by its proper instruments first, and then by some more special considerations or arguments of content.

1. When any thing happens to our displeasure, let us endeavour to take off its trouble by turning it into spiritual or artificial advantage, and handle it on that side in which it may be useful to the designs of reason; for there is nothing but hath a double handle, or at least we have two hands to apprehend it. When an enemy reproaches us; let us look on him as an impartial relator of our faults, for he will tell thee truer than thy fondest friend will; and thou mayest call them precious balms, though they break thy head, and forgive his anger, while thou makest use of the plainness of his declamation. "The ox, when he is weary, treads surest", and if there be nothing else in the disgrace but that it makes us to walk warily, and tread sure for fear of our enemies, that is better than to be flattered into pride and carelessness. This is the charity of Christian philosophy, which expounds the sense of the divine providence fairly, and reconciles us to it by a charitable construction: and we may as well refuse all physic, if we consider it only as unpleasant in the taste; and we may find fault with the rich valleys of Thasus, because they are circled by sharp mountains: but so also we may be in charity with every unpleasant accident, because, though it taste bitter, it is intended for health and medicine.

If therefore thou fallest from thy employment in public, take sanctuary in an honest retirement, being indifferent to thy gain abroad, or thy safety at home. If thou art out of favour with thy prince, secure the favour of the King of kings, and then there is no harm come to thee. And when Zeno Citiensis lost all his goods in a storm, he retired to the studies of philosophy, to his short cloak and a severe life, and gave thanks to fortune for his prosperous mischance. When the north wind blows hard, and it rains sadly, none but fools sit down in it and cry; wise people defend themselves against it with a warm garment, or a good fire and a dry roof. When a storm of a sad mischance beats upon our spirits, turn it into some advantage by observing where it can serve another end either of religion or prudence, of more safety or less envy: it will turn into something that is good, if we list to make it so; at least it may make us weary of the world's vanity, and take off our confidence from uncertain riches, and make our spirits to dwell in those regions where content dwells essentially. If it does any good to our souls, it hath made more than sufficient recompense for all the temporal affliction. He that threw a stone at a dog and hit his cruel step-mother, said that although he intended it otherwise, yet the stone was not quite lost: and if we fail in the first design, if we bring it home to another equally to content us, or more to profit us, then we have put our conditions past the power of chance; and this was called, in the old Greek comedy, "a being revenged on fortune by becoming philosophers", and turning the chance into reason or religion: for so a wise man shall overrule his stars, and have a greater influence upon his own content than all the constellations and planets of the firmament.

2. Never compare thy condition with those above thee; but, to secure thy content, look upon those thousands with whom thou wouldst not for any interest change thy fortune and condition. A soldier must not think himself unprosperous, if he be not successful as the son of Philip, or cannot grasp a fortune as big as the Roman empire. Be content, that thou art not lessened as was Pyrrhus; or if thou beest, that thou art not routed like Crassus: and when that comes to thee, it is a great prosperity that thou art not caged and made a spectacle, like Bajazet, or thy eyes were not pulled out, like Zedekiah's, or that thou were not flayed alive, like Valentinian. If thou admirest the greatness of Xerxes, look also on those that digged the mountain Atho, or whose ears and

noses were cut off because the Hellespont carried away the bridge. It is a fine thing, thou thinkest, to be carried on men's shoulders: but give God thanks that thou are not forced to carry a rich fool upon thy shoulders, as those poor men do whom thou beholdest. There are but a few kings in mankind; but many thousands who are very miserable, if compared to thee. However it is a huge folly rather to grieve for the good of others than to rejoice for that good which God hath given us of our own.

And yet there is no wise or good man that would change persons or conditions entirely with any man in the world. It may be he would have one man's wealth added to himself, or the power of a second, or the learning of a third; but still he would receive these into his own person, because he loves that best, and therefore esteems it best, and therefore over-values all that which he is before all that which any other man in the world can be. Would any man be Dives to have his wealth, or Judas for his office, or Saul for his kingdom, or Absalom for his beauty, or Achitophel for his policy? It is likely he would wish all these, and yet he would be the same person still. For every man hath desires of his own, and objects just fitted to them, without which he cannot be, unless he were not himself. And let every man that loves himself so well as to love himself before all the world, consider if he have not something for which in the whole he values himself far more than he can value any man else. There is therefore no reason to take the finest feathers from all the winged nation to deck that bird, that thinks already she is more valuable than any of the inhabitants of the air: either change all or none; cease to love yourself best, or be content with that portion of being and blessing for which you love yourself so well.

3. It conduces much to our content, if we pass by those things which happen to our trouble, and consider that which is pleasing and prosperous, that by the representation of the better the worse may be blotted out: and at the worst you have enough to keep you alive, and to keep up and to improve your hopes of heaven. If I be overthrown in my suit at law, yet my house is left me still and my land; or I have a virtuous wife, or hopeful children, or kind friends, or good hopes. If I have lost one child, it may be

I have two or three still left me. Or else reckon the blessings which already you have received, and therefore be pleased in the change and variety of affairs, to receive evil from the hand of God as well as good. Antipater of Tarsus used this art to support his sorrows on his deathbed, and reckoned the good things of his past life, not forgetting to recount it as a blessing, an argument that God took care of him, that he had a prosperous journey from Cilicia to Athens. Or else please thyself with hopes of the future: for we were not born with this sadness upon us; and it was a change that brought us into it, and a change may bring us out again. Harvest will come, and then every farmer is rich, at least for a month or two: it may be thou art entered into the cloud which will bring a gentle shower to refresh thy sorrows.

Now suppose thyself in as great a sadness as ever did load thy spirit, wouldst thou not bear it cheerfully and nobly if thou were sure that within a certain space some strange excellent fortune would relieve thee, and enrich thee, and recompense thee so as to overflow all thy hopes and thy desires and capacities? Now then, when a sadness lies heavy upon thee, remember that thou art a Christian designed to the inheritance of Jesus: and what dost thou think concerning thy great fortune, thy lot and portion of eternity? dost thou think thou shalt be saved or damned? Indeed if thou thinkest thou shalt perish, I cannot blame thee to be sad, sad till thy heart-strings crack: but then why art thou troubled at the loss of thy money? What should a damned man do with money, which in so great a sadness it is impossible for him to enjoy? Did ever any man upon the rack afflict himself because he had received a cross answer from his mistress? or call for the particulars of a purchase upon the gallows? If thou dost really believe thou shalt be damned, I do not say it will cure the sadness of thy poverty, but it will swallow it up. But if thou believest thou shalt be saved, consider how great is that joy, how infinite is that change, how unspeakable is the glory, how excellent is the recompense for all the sufferings in the world, if they were all laden upon the spirit? So that let thy condition be what it will, if thou considerest thy own present condition, and comparest it to thy future possibility, thou canst not feel the present smart of a cross fortune to any great degree, either because thou hast a far bigger sorrow, or a far bigger joy. Here thou art but a stranger travelling to thy country where the glories of a kingdom are prepared for thee; it is therefore a huge folly to be much afflicted because thou hast a less convenient inn to lodge in by the way.

But these arts of looking forwards and backwards are more than enough to support the spirit of a Christian: there is no man but hath blessings enough in present possession to outweigh the evils of a great affliction. Tell the joints of thy body, and do not accuse the universal providence for a lame leg, or the want of a finger, when all the rest is perfect, and you have a noble soul, a particle of divinity, the image of God himself: and by the want of a finger you may the better know how to estimate the remaining parts, and to account for every degree of the surviving blessings. Aristippus in a great suit at law lost a farm, and to a gentleman who in civility pitied and deplored his loss he answered, "I have two farms left still, and that is more than I have lost, and more than you have by one". If you miss an office for which you stood candidate, then, besides that you are quit of the cares and the envy of it, you still have all those excellencies which rendered you capable to receive it, and they are better than the best office in the commonwealth. If your estate be lessened, you need the less to care who governs the province, whether he be rude or gentle. I am crossed in my journey, and yet I escaped robbers; and I consider that if I had been set upon by villains, I would have redeemed that evil by this which I now suffer, and have counted it a deliverance: or if I did fall into the hands of thieves, yet they did not steal my land. Or I am fallen into the hands of publicans and sequestrators, and they have taken all from me: what now? let me look about me. They have left me the sun and moon, fire and water, a loving wife, and many friends to pity me, and some to relieve me, and I can still discourse; and unless I list they have not taken away my merry countenance, and my cheerful spirit, and a good conscience: they still have left me the providence of God, and all the promises of the gospel, and my religion, and my hopes of heaven, and my charity to them too;

and still I sleep and digest, I eat and drink, I read and meditate, I can walk in my neighbour's pleasant fields, and see the varieties of natural beauties, and delight in all that in which God delights, that is, in virtue and wisdom, in the whole creation, and in God himself. And he that hath so many causes of joy and so great, is very much in love with sorrow and peevishness, who loses all these pleasures, and chooses to sit down upon his little handful of thorns. Such a person were fit to bear Nero company in his funeral sorrow for the loss of one of Poppea's hairs, or help to mourn for Lesbia's sparrow: and because he loves it, he deserves to starve in the midst of plenty, and to want comfort while he is encircled with blessings.

4. Enjoy the present whatsoever it be, and be not solicitous for the future; for if you take your foot from the present standing, and thrust it forward towards to-morrow's event, you are in a restless condition; it is like refusing to quench your present thirst, by fearing you shall want drink the next day. If it be well to-day, it is madness to make the present miserable by fearing it may be ill to-morrow; when your belly is full of to-day's dinner, to fear you shall want the next day's supper: for it may be you shall not, and then to what purpose was this day's affliction? But if to-morrow you shall want, your sorrow will come time enough though you do not hasten it; let your trouble tarry till its own day comes. But if it chance to be ill to-day, do not increase it by the care of to-morrow: enjoy the blessings of this day, if God sends them, and the evils of it bear patiently and sweetly: for this day is only ours; we are dead to yesterday, and we are not yet born to the morrow; he therefore that enjoys the present if it be good, enjoys as much as is possible; and if only that day's trouble leans upon him, it is singular and finite. "Sufficient to the day", said Christ, "is the evil thereof": sufficient, but not intolerable; but if we look abroad, and bring into one day's thoughts the evil of many, certain and uncertain, what will be and what will never be, our load will be as intolerable as it is unreasonable. To reprove this instrument of discontent, the ancients feigned that in hell stood a man twisting a rope of hay; and still he twisted on, suffering an ass to eat up all that was

finished: so miserable is he who thrusts his passions forwards towards future events, and suffers all that he may enjoy to be lost and devoured by folly and inconsideration, thinking nothing fit to be enjoyed but that which is not, or cannot be had. Just so, many young persons are loath to die, and therefore desire to live to old age, and when they are come thither, are troubled that they are come to that state of life to which before they were come they were hugely afraid they should never come.

6. Let us prepare our minds against changes, always expecting them, that we be not surprised when they come: for nothing is so great an enemy to tranquillity and a contented spirit as the amazement and confusions of unreadiness and inconsideration; and when our fortunes are violently changed, our spirits are unchanged if they always stood in the suburbs and expectation of sorrows. "O death, how bitter art thou to a man, that is at rest in his possessions!" [Ecclus. xli. 1]. And to the rich man who had promised to himself ease and fulness for many years, it was a sad arrest that his soul was surprised the first night: but the apostles, who every day knocked at the gate of death, and looked upon it continually, went to their martyrdom in peace and evenness.

6. Let us often frame to ourselves and represent to our considerations the images of those blessings we have, just as we usually understand them when we want them. Consider how desirable health is to a sick man, or liberty to a prisoner; and if but a fit of the toothache seizes us with violence, all those troubles, which in our health afflicted us, disband instantly, and seem inconsiderable. He that in his health is troubled that he is in debt, and spends sleepless nights, and refuses meat because of his infelicity, let him fall into a fit of the stone or a high fever, he despises the arrest of all his first troubles, and is as a man unconcerned. Remember then that God hath given thee a blessing, the want of which is infinitely more trouble than thy present debt or poverty or loss; and therefore is now more to be valued in the possession, and ought to outweigh thy trouble. The very privative blessings, the blessings of immunity, safeguard, liberty, and integrity, which we commonly enjoy, deserve the thanksgiving of a

whole life. If God should send a cancer upon thy face or a wolf into thy side, if he should spread a crust of leprosy upon thy skin, what wouldst thou give to be but as now thou art? Wouldst thou not, on that condition, be as poor as I am, or as the meanest of thy brethren? Would you not choose your present loss or affliction as a thing extremely eligible, and a redemption to thee, if thou mightest exchange the other for this? Thou art quit from a thousand calamities, every one of which if it were upon thee would make thee insensible of thy present sorrow: and therefore let thy joy, which should be as great for thy freedom from them as is thy sadness when thou feelest any of them, do the same cure upon thy discontent. For if we be not extremely foolish or vain, thankless or senseless, a great joy is more apt to cure sorrow and discontent than a great trouble is. I have known an affectionate wife, when she hath been in fear of parting with her beloved husband, heartily desire of God his life or society upon any conditions that were not sinful, and choose to beg with him rather than to feast without him; and the same person hath upon that consideration borne poverty nobly, when God hath heard her prayer in the other matter. What wise man in the world is there who does not prefer a small fortune with peace before a great one with contention, and war, and violence? and then he is no longer wise, if he alters his opinion when he hath his wish.

7. If you will secure a contented spirit, you must measure your desires by your fortune and condition, not your fortunes by your desires: that is, be governed by your needs, not by your fancy; by nature, not by evil customs and ambitious principles. He that would shoot an arrow out of a plough, or hunt a hare with an elephant, is not unfortunate for missing the mark or prey: but he is foolish for choosing such unapt instruments: and so is he, that runs after his content with appetites not springing from natural needs, but from artificial, fantastical, and violent necessities. These are not to be satisfied; or if they were, a man hath chosen an evil instrument towards his content: nature did not intend rest to a man by filling of such desires. Is that beast better, that hath two or three mountains to graze on, than a little bee that feeds on dew or manna, and lives upon what falls every

morning from the storehouses of heaven, clouds and providence? can a man quench his thirst better out of a river than a full urn, or drink better from the fountain when it is finely paved with marble, than when it swells over the green turf? Pride and artificial gluttonies do but adulterate nature, making our diet healthless, our appetites impatient and unsatisfiable, and the taste mixed, fantastical, and meretricious. But that which we miscall poverty is indeed nature, and its proportions are the just measures of a man, and the best instruments of content; but when we create needs that God or nature never made, we have erected to ourselves an infinite stock of trouble that can have no period. Sempronius complained of want of clothes, and was much troubled for a new suit, being ashamed to appear in the theatre with his gown a little threadbare: but when he got it, and gave his old clothes to Codrus, the poor man was ravished with joy, and went and gave God thanks for his new purchase; and Codrus was made richly fine and cheerfully warm by that which Sempronius was ashamed to wear: and yet their natural needs were both alike; the difference only was that Sempronius had some artificial and fantastical necessities superinduced which Codrus had not, and was harder to be relieved, and could not have joy at so cheap a rate; because he only lived according to nature, the other by pride and ill customs, and measures taken by other men's eyes and tongues, and artificial needs. He that propounds to his fancy things greater than himself or his needs, and is discontent and troubled when he fails of such purchases, ought not to accuse Providence, or blame his fortune, but his folly. God and nature made no more needs than they mean to satisfy; and he that will make more must look for satisfaction where he can.

8. In all troubles and sadder accidents, let us take sanctuary in religion, and by innocence cast out anchors for our souls, to keep them from shipwreck though they be not kept from storm. For what philosophy shall comfort a villain that is haled to the rack for murdering his prince, or that is broken upon the wheel for sacrilege? His cup is full of pure and unmingled sorrow; his body is rent with torment, his name with ignominy, his soul with shame and sorrow which are to last eternally. But when a man

suffers in a good cause, or is afflicted, and yet walks not perversely with his God, then "Anytus and Melitus may kill me, but they cannot hurt me": then St. Paul's character is engraved in the forehead of our fortune, "we are troubled on every side, but not distressed; perplexed, but not in despair; persecuted, but not forsaken; cast down, but not destroyed" [2 Cor. iv. 8,9]; "and who is he that will harm you, if ye be followers of that which is good?" [1 Peter iii. 3; iv. 15,16]. For indeed every thing in the world is indifferent, but sin: and all the scorchings of the sun are very tolerable in respect of the burnings of a fever or a calenture. The greatest evils are from within us: and from ourselves also we must look for our greatest good; for God is the fountain of it, but reaches it to us by our own hands: and when all things look sadly round about us, then only we shall find, how excellent a fortune it is to have God to our friend; and, of all friendships, that only is created to support us in our needs. For it is sin that turns an ague into a fever, and a fever to the plague, fear into despair, anger into rage, and loss into madness, and sorrow to amazement and confusion: but if either we were innocent, or else by the sadness are made penitent, we are put to school, or into the theatre, either to learn how, or else actually to combat for a crown; the accident may serve an end of mercy, but is not a messenger of wrath.

Let us not therefore be governed by external, and present, and seeming things; nor let us make the same judgment of things that common and weak understandings do; nor make other men, and they not the wisest, to be judges of our felicity, so that we be happy or miserable as they please to think us: but let reason, and experience, and religion, and hope relying upon the divine promises, be the measure of our judgment. No wise man did ever describe felicity without virtue, and no good man did ever think virtue could depend upon the variety of a good or bad fortune. It is no evil to be poor, but to be vicious and impatient.

7 RULES AND MEASURES OF JUSTICE IN BARGAINING

1. In making contracts, use not many words; for all the business of a bargain is summed up in few sentences: and he that speaks least, means fairest, as having fewer opportunities to deceive.

2. Lie not at all, neither in a little thing nor in a great, neither in the substance nor in the circumstance, neither in word nor deed; that is, pretend not what is false, cover not what is true: and let the measure of your affirmation or denial be the understanding of your contractor; for he that deceives the buyer or the seller by speaking what is true in a sense not intended or understood by the other, is a liar and a thief; for in bargains you are to avoid not only what is false, but that also which deceives.

3. In prices of bargaining concerning uncertain merchandises, you may buy as cheap ordinarily as you can, and sell as dear as you can, so it be, first, without violence; and secondly, when you contract on equal terms with persons in all senses, as to the matter and skill of bargaining, equal to yourself, that is, merchants with merchants, wise men with wise men, rich with rich; and thirdly, when there is no deceit, and no necessity, and no monopoly: for in these cases, viz., when the contractors are equal, and no advantage on either side, both parties are voluntary, and therefore there can be no injustice or wrong to either. But then add also this consideration, that the public be not oppressed by unreasonable and unjust rates: for which the following rules are the best measure.

4. Let your prices be according to that measure of good and evil which is established in the fame and common accounts of the wisest and most merciful men, skilled in that manufacture or commodity; and the gain such which without scandal is allowed to persons in all the same circumstances.

5. Let no prices be heightened by the necessity or unskilfulness of the contractor: for the first is direct uncharitableness to the person, and injustice in the thing, because the man's necessity could not naturally enter into the consideration of the value of the commodity; and the other is deceit and oppression: much less must any man make necessities, as by engrossing a commodity,

by monopoly, by detaining corn, or the like indirect arts; for such persons are unjust to all single persons with whom in such cases they contract, and oppressors of the public.

6. In intercourse with others, do not do all which you may lawfully do, but keep something within thy power: and because there is a latitude of gain in buying and selling, take not thou the utmost penny that is lawful, or which thou thinkest so; for although it be lawful, yet it is not safe; and he that gains all that he can gain lawfully this year, possibly next year will be tempted to gain something unlawfully.

7. He that sells dearer by reason he sells not for ready money, must increase his price no higher than to make himself recompense for the loss which according to the rules of trade he sustained by his forbearance, according to common computation; reckoning in also the hazard, which he is prudently, warily, and charitably, to estimate. But although this be the measure of his justice, yet because it happens either to their friends, or to necessitous and poor persons, they are in these cases to consider the rules of friendship and neighbourhood, and the obligations of charity, lest justice turn into unmercifulness.

8. No man is to be raised in his price or rents in regard of any accident, advantage, or disadvantage, of his person: a prince must be used conscionably as well as a common person, and a beggar be treated justly as well as a prince; with this only difference, that to poor persons the utmost measure and extent of justice is unmerciful, which to a rich person is innocent, because it is just, and he needs not thy mercy and remission.

9. Let no man for his own poverty become more oppressing and cruel in his bargain, but quietly, modestly, diligently, and patiently, recommend his estate to God, and follow its interest, and leave the success to Him: for such courses will more probably advance his trade; they will certainly procure him a blessing and a recompense, and if they cure not his poverty, they will take away the evil of it; and there is nothing else in it that can trouble him.

10. Detain not the wages of the hireling, for every degree of detention of it beyond the time is injustice and uncharitableness,

and grinds his face till tears and blood come out; but pay him exactly according to covenant, or according to his needs.

11. Religiously keep all promises and covenants though made to your disadvantage, though afterwards you perceive you might have been better; and let not any precedent act of yours be altered by any after accident. Let nothing make you break your promise, unless it be unlawful, or impossible; that is, either out of your natural, or out of your civil power, yourself being under the power of another; or that it be intolerably inconvenient to yourself, and of no advantage to another; or that you have leave expressed, or reasonably presumed.

12. Let no man take wages or fees for a work that he cannot do, or cannot with probability undertake, or in some sense profitably and with ease or with advantage manage. Physicians must not meddle with desperate diseases, and known to be incurable, without declaring their sense beforehand; that if the patient please, he may entertain him at adventure, or to do him some little ease. Advocates must deal plainly with their clients, and tell them the true state and danger of their case, and must not pretend confidence in an evil cause; but when he hath so cleared his own innocence, if the client will have collateral and legal advantages obtained by his industry, he may engage his endeavour, provided he do no injury to the right cause, or any man's person.

13. Let no man appropriate to his own use what God by a special mercy, or the republic, hath made common; for that is both against justice and charity too. And by miraculous accidents God hath declared His displeasure against such enclosure: when the kings of Naples enclosed the gardens of Œnotria where the best manna of Calabria descends, that no man might gather it without paying tribute, the manna ceased till the tribute was taken off, and then it came again; and so when after the third trial the princes found they could not have that in proper which God made to be common, they left it as free as God gave it. The like happened in Epire; when Lysimachus laid an impost upon the Tragasean salt, it vanished, till Lysimachus left it public. And when the procurators of King Antigonus imposed a rate upon the sick people that came to Edepsum to drink the waters which

were lately sprung, and were very healthful, instantly the waters dried up, and the hope of gain perished.

The sum of all is in these words of St. Paul, "Let no man go beyond and defraud his brother in any matter, because the Lord is the avenger of all such" [1 Thess. iv. 6]: and our blessed Saviour, in the enumerating the duties of justice, besides the commandment of, "Do not steal", adds, "Defraud not", forbidding, as a distinct explication of the old law, the tacit and secret theft of abusing our brother in civil contracts [Lev. xix. 13; 1 Cor. vi. 8; Matthew x. 9]. And it needs no other arguments to enforce this caution, but only that the Lord hath undertaken to avenge all such persons: and as He always does it in the great day of recompenses, so very often He does it here, by making the unclean portion of injustice to be as a canker-worm eating up all the other increase: it procures beggary, and a declining estate, or a caitiff cursed spirit, an ill name, the curse of the injured and oppressed person, and a fool or a prodigal to be his heir.

8 OF FAITH

The acts and offices of faith are,

1. To believe every thing which God hath revealed to us, and when once we are convinced that God hath spoken it, to make no further enquiry, but humbly to submit; ever remembering that there are some things which our understanding cannot fathom, nor search out their depth.

2. To believe nothing concerning God but what is honourable and excellent, as knowing that belief to be no honouring of God, which entertains of Him any dishonourable thoughts. Faith is the parent of charity, and whatsoever faith entertains must be apt to produce love to God; but he that believes God to be cruel or unmerciful, or a rejoicer in the unavoidable damnation of the greatest part of mankind, or that He speaks one thing and privately means another, thinks evil thoughts concerning God, and

such as for which we should hate a man, and therefore are great enemies of faith, being apt to destroy charity. Our faith concerning God must be as Himself hath revealed and described His own excellencies, and in our discourses we must remove from Him all imperfection, and attribute to Him all excellency.

3. To give ourselves wholly up to Christ in heart and desire, to become disciples of His doctrine with choice (besides conviction), being in the presence of God but as idiots, that is, without any principles of our own to hinder the truth of God; but sucking in greedily all that God hath taught us, believing it infinitely, and loving to believe it. For this is an act of love, reflected upon faith; or an act of faith, leaning upon love.

4. To believe all God's promises, and that whatsoever is promised in scripture shall on God's part be as surely performed as if we had it in possession; this act makes us to rely upon God with the same confidence as we did on our parents when we were children, when we made no doubt but whatsoever we needed we should have it if it were in their power.

5. To believe also the conditions of the promise, or that part of the revelation which concerns our duty. Many are apt to believe the article of remission of sins, but they believe it without the condition of repentance, or the fruits of holy life; and that is to believe the article otherwise than God intended it. For the covenant of the gospel is the great object of faith, and that supposes our duty to answer His grace; that God will be our God so long as we are His people: the other is not faith, but flattery.

6. To profess publicly the doctrine of Jesus Christ, openly owning whatsoever He hath revealed and commanded, not being ashamed of the word of God, or of any practices enjoined by it; and this, without complying with any man's interest, not regarding favour, nor being moved with good words, not fearing disgrace, or loss, or inconvenience, or death itself.

7. To pray without doubting, without weariness, without faintness, entertaining no jealousies or suspicions of God, but being confident of God's hearing us, and of His returns to us, whatsoever the manner or the instance be, that if we do our duty it will be gracious and merciful.

These acts of faith are in several degrees in the servants of Jesus; some have it but as a grain of mustard seed, some grow up to a plant, some have the fulness of faith; but the least faith that is, must be a persuasion so strong as to make us undertake the doing of all that duty which Christ built upon the foundation of believing. But we shall best discern the truth of our faith by these following signs. St. Jerome reckons three;–

Signs of true faith

1. An earnest and vehement prayer; for it is impossible we should heartily believe the things of God and the glories of the gospel, and not most importunately desire them. For every thing is desired according to our belief of its excellency and possibility.

2. To do nothing for vain glory, but wholly for the interests of religion, and these articles we believe; valuing not at all the rumours of men, but the praise of God, to whom by faith we have given up all our intellectual faculties.

3. To be content with God for our judge, for our patron, for our Lord, for our friend; desiring God to be all in all to us, as we are in our understanding and affections wholly His. – Add to these,

4. To be a stranger upon earth in our affections, and to have all our thoughts and principal desires fixed upon the matters of faith, the things of heaven. For if a man were adopted heir to Cæsar, he would, if he believed it real and effective, despise the present, and wholly be at court in his father's eye; and his desires would outrun his swiftest speed, and all his thoughts would spend themselves in creating ideas and little fantastic images of his future condition. Now God hath made us heirs of His kingdom, and co-heirs with Jesus; if we believed this, we would think, and affect, and study accordingly. But he that rejoices in gain, and his heart dwells in the world, and is espoused to a fair estate, and transported with a light momentany joy, and is afflicted with losses, and amazed with temporal persecutions, and esteems disgrace or poverty in a good cause to be intolerable; this man either hath no inheritance in heaven, or believes none, and believes

not that he is adopted to be the son of God, the heir of eternal glory.

5. St. James's sign is the best, "Shew me thy faith by thy works". Faith makes the merchant diligent and venturous, and that makes him rich. Ferdinando of Arragon believed the story told him by Columbus, and therefore he furnished him with ships, and got the West Indies by his faith in the undertaker; but Henry the seventh of England believed him not, and therefore trusted him not with shipping, and lost all the purchase of that faith. It is told us by Christ, "he that forgives shall be forgiven": if we believe this, it is certain we shall forgive our enemies; for none of us all but need and desire to be forgiven. No man can possibly despise, or refuse to desire, such excellent glories as are revealed to them that are servants of Christ, and yet we do nothing that is commanded us as a condition to obtain them. No man could work a day's labour without faith; but because he believes he shall have his wages at the day's or week's end, he does his duty. But he only believes, who does that thing which other men in the like cases do when they do believe. He that believes money gotten with danger is better than poverty with safety, will venture for it in unknown lands or seas; and so will he that believes it better to get heaven with labour than to go to hell with pleasure.

6. He that believes does not make haste, but waits patiently till the times of refreshment come, and dares trust God for the morrow, and is no more solicitous for the next year than he is for that which is past: and it is certain that man wants faith, who dares be more confident of being supplied when he hath money in his purse, than when he hath it only in bills of exchange from God; or that relies more upon his own industry, than upon God's providence when his own industry fails him. If you dare trust to God when the case to human reason seems impossible, and trust to God then also out of choice, not because you have nothing else to trust to, but because He is the only support of a just confidence, then you give a good testimony of your faith.

7. True faith is confident, and will venture all the world upon the strength of its persuasion. Will you lay your life on it, your estate, your reputation, that the doctrine of Jesus Christ is true in

every article? then you have true faith. But he that fears men more than God, believes men more than he believes in God.

8. Faith, if it be true, living, and justifying, cannot be separated from a good life: it works miracles, makes a drunkard become sober, a lascivious person become chaste, a covetous man become liberal; it "overcomes the world", it "works righteousness" [2 Cor. xii. 5; Romans viii. 10], and it makes us diligently to do, and cheerfully to suffer, whatsoever God hath placed in our way to heaven.

The means and instruments to obtain faith are,

1. A humble, willing, and docible mind, or desire to be instructed in the way of God: for persuasion enters like a sunbeam, gently and without violence; and open but the window, and draw the curtain, and the Sun of righteousness will enlighten your darkness.

2. Remove all prejudice and love to every thing which may be contradicted by faith. "How can ye believe", said Christ, "that receive praise one of another?" An unchaste man cannot easily be brought to believe that without purity he shall never see God; he that loves riches can hardly believe the doctrine of poverty and renunciation of the world; and alms and martyrdom and the doctrine of the cross is folly to him that loves his ease and pleasures: he that hath within him any principle contrary to the doctrines of faith, cannot easily become a disciple.

3. Prayer, which is instrumental to every thing, hath a particular promise in this thing: "he that lacks wisdom, let him ask it of God"; and "if you give good things to your children, how much more shall your heavenly Father give His spirit to them that ask Him?"

4. The consideration of the divine omnipotence and infinite wisdom, and our own ignorance, are great instruments of curing all doubting, and silencing the murmurs of infidelity.

5. Avoid all curiosity of enquiry into particulars and circumstances and mysteries: for true faith is full of ingenuity and hearty simplicity, free from suspicion, wise and confident, trusting upon

generals, without watching and prying into unnecessary or indiscernible particulars. No man carries his bed into his field to watch how his corn grows, but believes upon the general order of providence and nature; and at harvest finds himself not deceived.

6. In time of temptation, be not busy to dispute, but rely upon the conclusion, and throw yourself upon God: and contend not with Him but in prayer, and in the presence and with the help of a prudent untempted guide; and be sure to esteem all changes of belief which offer themselves in the time of your greatest weakness, contrary to the persuasions of your best understanding, to be temptations, and reject them accordingly.

7. It is a prudent course that in our health and best advantages we lay up particular arguments and instruments of persuasion and confidence, to be brought forth and used in the great day of expense; and that especially in such things in which we use to be most tempted, and in which we are least confident, and which are most necessary, and which commonly the devil uses to assault us withal in the days of our visitation.

8. The wisdom of the church of God is very remarkable in appointing festivals or holy days, whose solemnity and offices have no other special business but to record the article of the day; such as Trinity sunday, Ascension, Easter, Christmas day; and to those persons who can only believe, not prove or dispute, there is no better instrument to cause the remembrance and plain notion, and to endear the affection and hearty assent to the article, than the proclaiming and recommending it by the festivity and joy of a holy day.

IV

Holy Dying

1 CONSIDERATION OF THE VANITY AND SHORTNESS OF MAN'S LIFE

A man is a bubble, said the Greek proverb; which Lucian represents with advantages and its proper circumstances, to this purpose; saying, that all the world is a storm, and men rise up in their several generations, like bubbles descending *a Jove pluvio*, from God and the dew of heaven, from a tear and drop of man, from nature and Providence: and some of these instantly sink into the deluge of their first parent, and are hidden in a sheet of water, having had no other business in the world but to be born that they might be able to die: others float up and down two or three turns, and suddenly disappear, and give their place to others: and they that live longest upon the face of the waters, are in perpetual motion, restless and uneasy; and being crushed with the great drop of a cloud sink into flatness and a froth; the change not being great, it being hardly possible it should be more a nothing that it was before. So is every man: he is born in vanity and sin; he comes into the world like morning mushrooms, soon thrusting up their heads into the air, and conversing with their kindred of the same production, and as soon they turn into dust and forgetfulness: some of them without any other interest in the affairs of the world but that they made their parents a little glad, and very sorrowful: others ride longer in the storm; it may be until seven years of vanity be expired, and then peradventure the sun shines hot upon their heads, and they fall into the shades below, into the cover of death and darkness of the grave to hide them. But if the bubble stands the shock of a bigger drop, and outlives the chances of a child, of a careless nurse, of drowning in a pail of water, of being overlaid by a sleepy servant, or such little accidents, then the young man dances like a bubble, empty and gay, and shines like a dove's neck, or the image of a rainbow, which hath no substance, and whose very imagery and colours are fantastical; and so he dances out the gaiety of his youth, and is all the while in a storm, and endures only because he is not knocked on the head by a drop of bigger rain, or crushed by the pressure of a load of indigested meat, or quenched by the disorder of an ill-placed humour: and to preserve a man alive in the midst of so many chances and hostilities, is as great a miracle as to create him; to preserve him from rushing into nothing, and at first to draw him up from nothing, were equally the issues of an almighty power. And therefore the wise men of the world have contended who shall best fit man's condition with words signifying his vanity and short abode. Homer calls a man "a leaf", the smallest, the weakest piece of a short-lived, unsteady plant: Pindar calls him "the dream of a shadow": another, "the dream of the shadow of smoke": but St. James spake by a more excellent spirit, saying, "our life is but a vapour" [James iv. 14] viz., drawn from the earth by a celestial influence; made of smoke, or the lighter parts of water, tossed with every wind, moved by the motion of a superior body, without virtue in itself, lifted up on high or left below, according as it pleases the sun its foster-father. But it is lighter yet; it is but "appearing"; a fantastic vapour, an apparition, nothing real: it is not so much as a mist, not the matter of a shower, nor substantial enough to make a cloud; but it is like Cassiopeia's chair, or Pelops' shoulder, or the circles of heaven, φαινομενα, than which you cannot have a word that can signify a verier nothing. And yet the expression is one degree more made diminutive: a "vapour", and "fantastical", or a "mere appearance", and this but for a little while neither; the very dream, the phantasm disappears in a small time, "like the shadow that departeth"; or "like a tale that is told"; or "as a dream, when one awaketh". A man is so vain, so unfixed, so perishing a creature, that he cannot long last in the scene of fancy: a man goes off, and is forgotten, like the dream of a distracted person. The sum of all is this: that thou art a man, than whom there is not in the world any greater instance of heights and declensions, of lights and shadows, of misery and folly, of laughter and tears, of groans and death.

And because this consideration is of great usefulness and great necessity to many purposes of wisdom and the spirit; all the succession of time, all the changes in nature, all the varieties of light and darkness, the thousand thousands of accidents in the world, and every contingency to every man, and to every creature, doth preach our funeral sermon, and calls us to look and see how the old sexton Time throws up the earth, and digs a grave where we must lay our sins or our sorrows, and sow our bodies, till they rise again in a fair or in an intolerable eternity. Every revolution which the sun makes about the world, divides between life and death; and death possesses both those portions by the next morrow; and we are dead to all those months which we have already lived, and we shall never live them over again: and still God makes little periods of our age. First we change our world, when we come from the womb to feel the warmth of the sun. Then we sleep and enter into the image of death, in which state we are unconcerned in all the changes of the world: and if our mothers or our nurses die, or a wild boar destroy our vineyards, or our king be sick, we regard it not, but during that state are as disinterest as if our eyes were closed with the clay that weeps in the bowels of the earth. At the end of seven years our teeth fall and die before us, representing a formal prologue to the tragedy; and still every seven years it is odds but we shall finish the last scene: and when nature, or chance, or vice, takes our body in pieces, weakening some parts and loosing others, we taste the grave and the solemnities of our own funerals, first in those parts that ministered to vice, and next in them that served for ornament, and in a short time even they that served for necessity become useless, and entangled like the wheels of a broken clock. Baldness is but a dressing to our funerals, the proper ornament of mourning, and of a person entered very far into the regions and possession of death: and we have many more of the same signification; gray hairs, rotten teeth, dim eyes, trembling joints, short breath, stiff limbs, wrinkled skin, short memory, decayed appetite. Every day's necessity calls for a reparation of that portion which death fed on all night, when we lay in his lap, and slept in his outer chambers. The very spirits of a man prey upon the daily portion of bread and flesh, and every meal is a rescue from one death, and lays up for another; and while we think a thought, we die; and the clock strikes, and reckons on our portion of eternity: we form our words with the breath of our nostrils, we have the less to live upon for every word we speak.

Thus nature calls us to meditate of death by those things which are the instruments of acting it: and God by all the variety of His providence makes us see death every where, in all variety of circumstances, and dressed up for all the fancies and the expectation of every single person. Nature hath given us one harvest every year, but death hath two, and the spring and the autumn send throngs of men and women to charnel-houses; and all the summer long men are recovering from their evils of the spring, till the dog days come, and then the Sirian star makes the summer deadly; and the fruits of autumn are laid up for all the year's provision, and the man that gathers them eats and surfeits, and dies and needs them not, and himself is laid up for eternity; and he that escapes till winter only stays for another opportunity which the distempers of that quarter minister to him with great variety. Thus death reigns in all the portions of our time; the autumn with its fruits provides disorders for us, and the winter's cold turns them into sharp diseases, and the spring brings flowers to strew our hearse, and the summer gives green turf and brambles to bind upon our graves. Calentures and surfeit, cold and agues, are the four quarters of the year, and all minister to death; and you can go no whither but you tread upon a dead man's bones.

The wild fellow in Petronius that escaped upon a broken table from the furies of a shipwreck, as he was sunning himself upon the rocky shore espied a man rolling upon his floating bed of waves, ballasted with sand in the folds of his garment, and carried by his civil enemy, the sea, towards the shore to find a grave: and it cast him into some sad thoughts: that peradventure this man's wife in some part of the continent, safe and warm, looks next month for the good man's return; or, it may be, his son knows nothing of the tempest; or his father thinks of that affectionate kiss, which still is warm upon the good old man's cheek, ever since he took a kind farewell; and he weeps with joy to think how blessed he shall be when his beloved boy returns into the circle of his father's arms. These are the thoughts of mortals, this is the end and sum of all their designs: a dark night and an ill guide, a boisterous sea and a broken cable, a hard rock and a rough wind, dashed in pieces the fortune of a whole family, and they that shall weep loudest for the accident are not yet entered into the storm, and yet have suffered shipwreck. Then looking upon the carcass, he knew it, and found it to be the master of the ship, who the day before cast up the accounts of his patrimony and his trade, and named the day when he thought to be at home; see how the man swims who was so angry two days since; his passions are becalmed with the storm, his accounts cast up, his cares at an end, his voyage done, and his gains are the strange events of death, which whether they be good or evil, the men that are alive seldom trouble themselves concerning the interest of the dead.

But seas alone do not break our vessel in pieces: every where we may be shipwrecked. A valiant general, when he is to reap the harvest of his crowns and triumphs, fights unprosperously; or falls into a fever with joy and wine, and changes his laurel into cypress, his triumphal chariot to a hearse, dying the night before he was appointed to perish in the drunkenness of his festival joys. It was a sad arrest of the loosenesses and wilder feasts of the French court, when their king Henry the Second was killed really by the sportive image of a fight. And many brides have died under the hands of paranymphs and maidens, dressing them for uneasy joy, the new and undiscerned chains of marriage, according to the saying of Bensirah, the wise Jew, "the bride went into her chamber, and knew not what should befal her there". Some have been paying their vows, and giving thanks for a prosperous return to their own house, and the roof hath descended upon their heads, and turned their loud religion into the deeper silence of a grave. And how many teeming mothers have rejoiced over their swelling wombs, and pleased themselves in becoming the channels of blessing to a family, and the midwife hath quickly bound their heads and feet, and carried them forth to burial! Or else the birth-day of an heir hath seen the coffin of the father brought into the house, and the divided mother hath been forced to travail twice, with a painful birth, and a sadder death.

There is no state, no accident, no circumstance of our life, but it hath been soured by some sad instance of a dying friend: a friendly meeting often ends in some sad mischance, and makes an eternal parting: and when the poet Æschylus was sitting under the walls of his house, an eagle hovering over his bald head, mistook it for a stone, and let fall his oyster, hoping there to break the shell, but pierced the poor man's skull.

Death meets us every where, and is procured by every instrument and in all chances, and enters in at many doors; by violence and secret influence, by the aspect of a star and the stink of a mist, by the emissions of a cloud and the meeting of a vapour, by the fall of a chariot and the stumbling at a stone, by a full meal or an empty stomach, by watching at the wine or by watching at prayers, by the sun or the moon, by a heat or a cold, by sleepless nights or sleeping days, by water frozen into the hardness and sharpness of a dagger, or water thawed into the floods of a river, by a hair or a raisin, by violent motion or sitting still, by severity or dissolution, by God's mercy or God's anger; by every thing in providence and every thing in manners, by every thing in nature and every thing in chance.

Eripitur persona, manet res:
we take pains to heap up things useful to our life, and get our death in the purchase; and the person is snatched away, and the goods remain. And all this is the law and constitution of nature; it is a punishment to our sins, the unalterable event of providence, and the decree of heaven: the chains that confine us to this condition are strong as destiny, and immutable as the eternal laws of God.

I have conversed with some men who rejoiced in the death or calamity of others, and accounted it as a judgment upon them for being on the other side, and against them in the contention: but within the revolution of a few months, the same man met with a more uneasy and unhandsome death: which when I saw, I wept, and was afraid; for I knew that it must be so with all men; for we also shall die, and end our quarrels and contentions by passing to a final sentence.

2 CONSIDERATION OF THE MISERIES OF MAN'S LIFE

As our life is very short, so it is very miserable; and therefore it is well it is short. God in pity to mankind, lest his burden should be insupportable and his nature an intolerable load, hath reduced our state of misery to an abbreviature; and the greater our misery is, the less while it is like to last; the sorrows of a man's spirit being like ponderous weights, which by the greatness of their burden make a swifter motion, and descend into the grave to rest and ease our wearied limbs; for then only we shall sleep quietly, when those fetters are knocked off, which not only bound our souls in prison, but also ate the flesh till the very bones opened the secret garments of their cartilages, discovering their nakedness and sorrow.

1. Here is no place to sit down in, but you must rise as soon as you are set, for we have gnats in our chambers, and worms in our gardens, and spiders and flies in the palaces of the greatest kings. How few men in the world are prosperous! What an infinite number of slaves and beggars, of persecuted and oppressed people, fill all corners of the earth with groans, and heaven itself with weeping prayers and sad remembrances! How many provinces and kingdoms are afflicted by a violent war, or made desolate by popular diseases! Some whole countries are remarked with fatal evils, or periodical sicknesses. Grand Cairo in Egypt feels the plague every three years returning like a quartan ague, and destroying many thousands of persons. All the inhabitants of Arabia the desert are in continual fear of being buried in huge heaps of sand, and therefore dwell in tents and ambulatory houses, or retire to unfruitful mountains, to prolong an uneasy and wilder life. And all the countries round about the Adriatic sea feel such violent convulsions by tempests and intolerable

earthquakes, that sometimes whole cities find a tomb, and every man sinks with his own house made ready to become his monument, and his bed is crushed into the disorders of a grave. Was not all the world drowned at one deluge and breach of the divine anger; and shall not all the world again be destroyed by fire? Are there not many thousands that die every night, and that groan and weep sadly every day? But what shall we think of that great evil which for the sins of men God hath suffered to possess the greatest part of mankind? Most of the men that are now alive, or that have been living for many ages, are Jews, Heathens, or Turks; and God was pleased to suffer a base epileptic person, a villain and a vicious, to set up a religion which hath filled all the nearer parts of Asia, and much of Africa, and some part of Europe; so that the greatest number of men and women born in so many kingdoms and provinces are infallibly made Mahometans, strangers and enemies to Christ by whom alone we can be saved: this consideration is extremely sad, when we remember how universal and how great an evil it is, that so many millions of sons and daughters are born to enter into the possession of devils to eternal ages. These evils are the miseries of great parts of mankind, and we cannot easily consider more particularly the evils which happen to us, being the inseparable affections or incidents to the whole nature of man.

2. We find that all the women in the world are either born for barrenness, or the pains of childbirth, and yet this is one of our greatest blessings; but such indeed are the blessings of this world, we cannot be well with nor without many things. Perfumes make our heads ache, roses prick our fingers, and in our very blood, where our life dwells, is the scene under which nature acts many sharp fevers and heavy sicknesses. It were too sad if I should tell how many persons are afflicted with evil spirits, with spectres and illusions of the night; and that huge multitudes of men and women live upon man's flesh; nay, worse yet, upon the sins of men, upon the sins of their sons and of their daughters, and they pay their souls down for the bread they eat, buying this day's meal with the price of the last night's sin.

3. Or if you please in charity to visit a hospital, which is indeed a

map of the whole world, there you shall see the effects of Adam's sin, and the ruins of human nature; bodies laid up in heaps like the bones of a destroyed town, *homines precarii spiritus et male hærentis*, men whose souls seem to be borrowed, and are kept there by art and the force of medicine, whose miseries are so great that few people have charity or humanity enough to visit them, fewer have the heart to dress them, and we pity them in civility or with a transient prayer, but we do not feel their sorrows by the mercies of a religious pity; and therefore as we leave their sorrows in many degrees unrelieved and uneased, so we contract by our unmercifulness a guilt by which ourselves become liable to the same calamities. Those many that need pity, and those infinities of people that refuse to pity, are miserable upon a several charge, but yet they almost make up all mankind.

4. All wicked men are in love with that which entangles them in huge varieties of troubles; they are slaves to the worst of masters, to sin and to the devil, to a passion, and to an imperious woman. Good men are for ever persecuted, and God chastises every son whom He receives, and whatsoever is easy is trifling, and worth nothing, and whatsoever is excellent is not to be obtained without labour and sorrow; and the conditions and states of men that are free from great cares are such as have in them nothing rich and orderly, and those that have are stuck full of thorns and trouble. Kings are full of care; and learned men in all ages have been observed to be very poor, *et honestas miserias accusant*, "they complain of their honest miseries".

5. But these evils are notorious and confessed; even they also whose felicity men stare at and admire, besides their splendour and the sharpness of their light, will with their appendant sorrows wring a tear from the most resolved eye; for not only the winter quarter is full of storms and cold and darkness, but the beauteous spring hath blasts and sharp frosts, the fruitful teeming summer is melted with heat, and burnt with the kisses of the sun her friend, and choked with dust, and the rich autumn is full of sickness; and we are weary of that which we enjoy, because sorrow is its biggest portion: and when we remember that upon the fairest face is placed one of the worst sinks of the body, the

nose, we may use it not only as a mortification to the pride of beauty, but as an allay to the fairest outside of condition which any of the sons and daughters of Adam do possess. For look upon kings and conquerors: I will not tell, that many of them fall into the condition of servants, and their subjects rule over them, and stand upon the ruins of their families, and that to such persons the sorrow is bigger than usually happens in smaller fortunes; but let us suppose them still conquerors, and see what a goodly purchase they get by all their pains, and amazing fears, and continual dangers. They carry their arms beyond Ister, and pass the Euphrates, and bind the Germans with the bounds of the river Rhine: I speak in the style of the Roman greatness; for now-a-days the biggest fortune swells not beyond the limits of a petty province or two, and a hill confines the progress of their prosperity, or a river checks it: but whatsoever tempts the pride and vanity of ambitious persons is not so big as the smallest star which we see scattered in disorder and unregarded upon the pavement and floor of heaven. And if we would suppose the pismires had but our understandings, they also would have the method of a man's greatness, and divide their little mole-hills into provinces and exarchates: and if they also grew as vicious and as miserable, one of their princes would lead an army out and kill his neighbour ants, that he might reign over the next handful of a turf. But then if we consider at what price and with what felicity all this is purchased, the sting of the painted snake will quickly appear, and the fairest of their fortunes will properly enter into this account of human infelicities.

We may guess at it by the constitution of Augustus's fortune, who struggled for his power first with the Roman citizens, then with Brutus and Cassius and all the fortune of the republic; then with his colleague Mark Antony; then with his kindred and nearest relatives; and after he was wearied with slaughter of the Romans, before he could sit down and rest in his imperial chair, he was forced to carry armies into Macedonia, Galatia, beyond Euphrates, Rhine, and Danubius; and when he dwelt at home in greatness and within the circles of a mighty power, he hardly escaped the sword of the Egnatii, of Lepidus, Cæpio, and Murena;

and after he had entirely reduced the felicity and grandeur into his own family, his daughter, his only child, conspired with many of the young nobility, and being joined with adulterous complications, as with an impious sacrament, they affrighted and destroyed the fortune of the old man, and wrought him more sorrow than all the troubles that were hatched in the baths and beds of Egypt between Antony and Cleopatra. This was the greatest fortune that the world had then or ever since, and therefore we cannot expect it to be better in a less prosperity.

6. The prosperity of this world is so infinitely soured with the overflowing of evils, that he is counted the most happy who hath the fewest; all conditions being evil and miserable, they are only distinguished by the number of calamities. The collector of the Roman and foreign examples, when he had reckoned two and twenty instances of great fortunes, every one of which had been allayed with great variety of evils; in all his reading or experience, he could tell but of two who had been famed for an entire prosperity, Quintus Metellus, and Gyges the king of Lydia: and yet concerning the one of them he tells that his felicity was so inconsiderable (and yet it was the bigger of the two) that the oracle said that Aglaus Sophidius the poor Arcadian shepherd was more happy than he, that is, he had fewer troubles; for so indeed we are to reckon the pleasures of this life; the limit of our joy is the absence of some degrees of sorrow, and he that hath the least of this, is the most prosperous person. But then we must look for prosperity not in palaces or courts of princes, not in the tents of conquerors, or in the gaieties of fortunate and prevailing sinners; but something rather in the cottages of honest, innocent, and contented persons, whose mind is no bigger than their fortune, nor their virtue less than their security. As for others, whose fortune looks bigger, and allures fools to follow it like the wandering fires of the night, till they run into rivers or are broken upon rocks with staring and running after them, they are all in the condition of Marius, than whose condition nothing was more constant, and nothing more mutable; if we reckon them amongst the happy, they are the most happy men; if we reckon them amongst the miserable, they are the most miserable. For just as

is a man's condition, great or little, so is the state of his misery; all have their share; but kings and princes, great generals and consuls, rich men and mighty, as they have the biggest business and the biggest charge, and are answerable to God for the greatest accounts, so they have the biggest trouble; that the uneasiness of their appendage may divide the good and evil of the world, making the poor man's fortune as eligible as the greatest; and also restraining the vanity of man's spirit, which a great fortune is apt to swell from a vapour to a bubble; but God in mercy hath mingled wormwood with their wine, and so restrained the drunkenness and follies of prosperity.

7. Man never hath one day to himself of entire peace from the things of this world, but either something troubles him, or nothing satisfies him, or his very fulness swells him and makes him breathe short upon his bed. Men's joys are troublesome, and besides that the fear of losing them takes away the present pleasure, and a man hath need of another felicity to preserve this, they are also wavering and full of trepidation, not only from their inconstant nature, but from their weak foundation: they arise from vanity, and they dwell upon ice, and they converse with the wind, and they have the wings of a bird, and are serious but as the resolutions of a child, commenced by chance, and managed by folly, and proceed by inadvertency, and end in vanity and forgetfulness. So that as Livius Drusus said of himself, he never had any play days or days of quiet when he was a boy, for he was troublesome and busy, a restless and unquiet man; the same may every man observe to be true of himself; he is always restless and uneasy, he dwells upon the waters, and leans upon thorns, and lays his head upon a sharp stone.

3 OF EXERCISING CHARITY DURING OUR WHOLE LIFE

He that would die well and happily must in his life-time according to all his capacities exercise charity; and because religion is the life of the soul, and charity is the life of religion, the same which gives life to the better part of man, which never dies, may obtain of God a mercy to the inferior part of man in the day of its dissolution.

1. Charity is the great channel through which God passes all His mercy upon mankind. For we receive absolution of our sins in proportion to our forgiving our brother: this is the rule of our hopes, and the measure of our desire in this world; and in the day of death and judgment the great sentence upon mankind shall be transacted according to our alms, which is the other part of charity. Certain it is that God cannot, will not, never did, reject a charitable man in his greatest needs and in his most passionate prayers; for God himself is love, and every degree of charity that dwells in us is the participation of the divine nature: and therefore when upon our death-bed a cloud covers our head, and we are enwrapped with sorrow; when we feel the weight of a sickness, and do not feel the refreshing visitations of God's loving-kindness; when we have many things to trouble us, and looking round about us we see no comforter; then call to mind what injuries you have forgiven, how apt you were to pardon all affronts and real persecutions, how you embraced peace when it was offered you, how you followed after peace when it ran from you: and when you are weary of one side, turn upon the other, and remember the alms that by the grace of God and His assistances you have done, and look up to God, and with the eye of faith behold Him coming in the cloud, and pronouncing the sentence of doomsday according to His mercies and thy charity.

2. Charity with its twin-daughters, alms and forgiveness, is especially effectual for the procuring God's mercies in the day and the manner of our death. "Alms deliver from death", said old Tobias [Tob. iv. 10; xii. 9] and, "alms make an atonement for sins", said the son of Sirach [Ecclus. iii. 30]: and so said Daniel [Dan. iv. 27], and so say all the wise men of the world. And in this sense also is that of St. Peter, "Love covers a multitude of sins" [1 Peter iv. 8; Isaiah i. 17]; and St. Clement in his Constitutions gives this counsel, "If you have any thing in your hands, give it, that it may work to the remission of thy sins: for by faith and alms sins are purged". The same also is the counsel of Salvian,

who wonders that men, who are guilty of great and many sins, will not work out their pardon by alms and mercy. But this also must be added out of the words of Lactantius, who makes this rule complete and useful; "But think not, because sins are taken away by alms, that by thy money thou mayest purchase a licence to sin: for sins are abolished, if because thou hast sinned thou givest to God", that is, to God's poor servants, and His indigent necessitous creatures: but "if thou sinnest upon confidence of giving, thy sins are not abolished. For God desires infinitely that men should be purged from their sins, and therefore commands us to repent; but to repent is nothing else but to profess and affirm (that is, to purpose, and to make good that purpose), that they will sin no more". Now alms are therefore effective to the abolition and pardon of our sins, because they are preparatory to, and impetratory of, the grace of repentance, and are fruits of repentance: and therefore St. Chrysostom affirms, that repentance without alms is dead, and without wings, and can never soar upwards to the element of love. But because they are a part of repentance, and hugely pleasing to Almighty God, therefore they deliver us from the evils of an unhappy and accursed death; for so Christ delivered His disciples from the sea, when He appeased the storm, though they still sailed in the channel: and this St. Jerome verifies with all his reading and experience, saying, "I do not remember to have read that ever any charitable person died an evil death". And although a long experience hath observed God's mercies to descend upon charitable people, like the dew upon Gideon's fleece, when all the world was dry; yet for this also we have a promise, which is not only an argument of a certain number of years, as experience is, but a security for eternal ages: "make ye friends of the mammon of unrighteousness, that when ye fail they may receive you into everlasting habitations". When faith fails, and chastity is useless, and temperance shall be no more, then charity shall bear you upon wings of cherubims to the eternal mountain of the Lord. "I have been a lover of mankind, and a friend, and merciful; and now I expect to communicate in that great kindness which He shews that is the great God and father of men and mercies", said Cyrus the Persian on his death-bed.

I do not mean this should only be a death-bed charity, any more than a death-bed repentance; but it ought to be the charity of our life and healthful years, a parting with portions of our goods then, when we can keep them: we must not first kindle our lights when we are to descend into our houses of darkness, or bring a glaring torch suddenly to a dark room, that will amaze the eye, and not delight it, or instruct the body; but if our tapers have, in their constant course, descended into their grave crowned all the way with light, then let the death-bed charity be doubled, and the light burn brightest when it is to deck our hearse. But concerning this I shall afterwards give account.

4 THE CIRCUMSTANCES OF A DYING MAN'S SORROW AND DANGER

When the sentence of death is decreed, and begins to be put in execution, it is sorrow enough to see or feel respectively the sad accents of the agony and last contentions of the soul, and the reluctances and unwillingnesses of the body: the forehead washed with a new and stranger baptism, besmeared with a cold sweat, tenacious and clammy, apt to make it cleave to the roof of his coffin; the nose cold and undiscerning, not pleased with perfumes, nor suffering violence with a cloud of unwholesome smoke; the eyes dim as a sullied mirror, or the face of heaven, when God shews His anger in a prodigious storm; the feet cold, the hands stiff, the physicians despairing, our friends weeping, the rooms dressed with darkness and sorrow, and the exterior parts betraying what are the violences which the soul and spirit suffer; the nobler part, like the lord of the house, being assaulted by exterior rudenesses, and driven from all the outworks, at last, faint and weary with short and frequent breathings, interrupted with the longer accents of sighs, without moisture but the excrescences of a spilt humour when the pitcher is broken at the cistern, it retires to its last fort, the heart; whither it is pursued, and stormed, and beaten out, as when the barbarous Thracian sacked the glory of the Grecian empire. Then calamity is great, and sorrow rules in all the capacities of man: then the mourners weep, because it is civil, or because they need thee, or because they fear: but who suffers for thee with a compassion sharp as is thy pain? Then the noise is like the faint echo of a distant valley, and few hear, and they will not regard thee, who seemest like a person void of understanding and of a departing interest. *Vere tremendum est mortis sacramentum.* But these accidents are common to all that die; and when a special providence shall distinguish them, they shall die with easy circumstances; but as no piety can secure it, so must no confidence expect it; but wait for the time, and accept the manner of the dissolution. But that which distinguishes them, is this:–

He that hath lived a wicked life, if his conscience be alarmed, and that he does not die like a wolf or a tiger, without sense or remorse of all his wildness and his injury, his beastly nature, and desert and untilled manners, if he have but sense of what he is going to suffer, or what he may expect to be his portion; then we may imagine the terror of their abused fancies, how they see affrighting shapes, and because they fear them, they feel the gripes of devils, urging the unwilling souls from the kinder and fast embraces of the body, calling to the grave and hastening to judgment, exhibiting great bills of uncancelled crimes, awaking and amazing the conscience, breaking all their hope in pieces, and making faith useless and terrible, because the malice was great, and the charity was none at all. Then they look for some to have pity on them, but there is no man. No man dares be their pledge: no man can redeem their soul, which now feels, what it never feared. Then the tremblings and the sorrow, the memory of the past sin, and the fear of future pains, and the sense of an angry God, and the presence of some devils, consign him to the eternal company of all the damned and accursed spirits. Then they want an angel for their guide, and the Holy Spirit for their comforter, and a good conscience for their testimony, and Christ for their advocate, and they die and are left in prisons of earth or air, in secret and undiscerned regions, to weep and tremble, and infinitely to fear the coming of the day of Christ; at which time they shall be brought forth to change their condition into a worse, where they shall for ever feel more than we can believe or understand.

But when a good man dies, one that hath lived innocently, or made joy in heaven at his timely and effective repentance, and in whose behalf the holy Jesus hath interceded prosperously, and for whose interest the Spirit makes interpellations with groans and sighs unutterable, and in whose defence the angels drive away the devils on his death-bed, because his sins are pardoned, and because he resisted the devil in his life-time, and fought successfully, and persevered unto the end; then the joys break forth through the clouds of sickness, and the conscience stands upright, and confesses the glories of God, and owns so much integrity, that it can hope for pardon, and obtain it too; then the sorrows of the sickness, and the flames of the fever, or the faintness of the consumption, do but untie the soul from its chain, and let it go forth, first into liberty, and then to glory: for it is but for a little while that the face of the sky was black, like the preparations of the night, but quickly the cloud was torn and rent, the violence of thunder parted it into little portions, that the sun might look forth with a watery eye, and then shine without a tear. But it is an infinite refreshment to remember all the comforts of his prayers, the frequent victory over his temptations, the mortification of his lust, the noblest sacrifice to God, in which He most delights, that we have given Him our wills, and killed our appetites for the interests of His services: then all the trouble of that is gone; and what remains is a portion in the inheritance of Jesus, of which he now talks no more as a thing at distance, but is entering into the possession. When the veil is rent, and the prison doors are open at the presence of God's angel, the soul goes forth full of hope, sometimes with evidence, but always with certainty in the thing, and instantly it passes into the throngs of spirits, where angels meet it singing, and the devils flock with malicious and vile purposes, desiring to lead it away with them into their houses of sorrow; there they see things which they never saw, and hear voices which they never heard. There the devils charge them with many sins, and the angels remember that themselves rejoiced when they were repented of. Then the devils aggravate and describe all the circumstances of the sin, and add calumnies; and the angels bear the soul forward still, because their Lord doth answer for them. Then the devils rage and gnash their teeth; they see the soul chaste and pure, and they are ashamed; they see it penitent, and they despair; they perceive that the tongue was refrained and sanctified, and then hold their peace. Then the soul passes forth and rejoices, passing by the devils in scorn and triumph, being securely carried into the bosom of the Lord, where they shall rest till their crowns are finished and their mansions are prepared; and then they shall feast and sing, rejoice and worship, for ever and ever. Fearful and formidable to unholy persons is the first meeting with spirits in their separation: but the victory which holy souls receive by the mercies of Jesus Christ and the conduct of angels, is a joy that we must not understand till we feel it; and yet such which by an early and a persevering piety we may secure; but let us enquire after it no further, because it is secret.

5 OF THE STATE OF SICKNESS

Adam's sin brought death into the world, and man did die the same day in which he sinned, according as God had threatened. He did not die, as death is taken for a separation of soul and body; that is not death properly, but the ending of the last act of death; just as a man is said to be born, when he ceases any longer to be borne in his mother's womb; but whereas to man was intended a life long and happy, without sickness, sorrow, or infelicity, and this life should be lived here or in a better place, and the passage from one to the other should have been easy, safe, and pleasant, now that man sinned, he fell from that state to a contrary.

If Adam had stood, he should not always have lived in this world; for this world was not a place capable of giving a dwelling to all those myriads of men and women, which should have been born in all the generations of infinite and eternal ages; for so it must have been, if man had not died at all, nor yet have removed hence at all. Neither is it likely that man's innocence should have lost to him all possibility of going thither, where the duration is better, measured by a better time, subject to fewer changes, and which is now the reward of a returning virtue, which in all natural senses is less than innocence, save that it is heightened by Christ to an equality of adaptation with the state of innocence: but so it must have been, that his innocence should have been punished with an eternal confinement to this state, which in all reason is the less perfect, the state of a traveller, not of one posssessed of his inheritance. It is therefore certain, man should have changed his abode: for so did Enoch, and so did Elias, and so shall all the world that shall be alive at the day of judgment; they shall not die, but they shall change their place and their abode, their duration and their state, and all this without death.

That death therefore which God threatened to Adam, and which passed upon his posterity, is not the going out of this world, but the manner of going. If he had stayed in innocence, he should have gone from hence placidly and fairly, without vexatious and afflictive circumstances; he should not have died in sickness, misfortune, defect, or unwillingness: but when he fell, then he began to die; the "same day", so said God, and that must needs be true: and therefore it must mean that upon that very day he fell into an evil and dangerous condition, a state of change and affliction; then death began, that is, the man began to die by a natural diminution, and aptness to disease and misery. His first state was, and should have been so long as it lasted, a happy duration; his second was a daily and miserable change, and this was the dying properly.

This appears in the great instance of damnation, which, in the style of scripture, is called eternal death: not because it kills or ends the duration; it hath not so much good in it; but because it is a perpetual infelicity. Change or separation of soul and body is but accidental to death; death may be with or without either: but the formality, the curse and the sting of death, that is, misery, sorrow, fear, diminution, defect, anguish, dishonour, and whatsoever is miserable and afflictive in nature, that is death. Death is not an action, but a whole state and condition; and this was first brought in upon us by the offence of one man.

But this went no farther than thus to subject us to temporal infelicity. If it had proceeded so as was supposed, man had been much more miserable; for man had more than one original sin, in this sense: and though this death entered first upon us by Adam's fault, yet it came nearer unto us and increased upon us by the sins of more of our forefathers. For Adam's sin left us in strength enough to contend with human calamities for almost a thousand years together: but the sins of his children, our forefathers, took off from us half the strength about the time of the flood; and then from five hundred to two hundred and fifty, and from thence to one hundred and twenty, and from thence to threescore and ten; so often halving of it, till it is almost come to nothing. But by the sins of men in the several generations of the world, death, that is, misery and disease, is hastened so upon us, that we are of a contemptible age: and because we are to die by suffering evils, and by the daily lessening of our strength and health; this death is so long a doing, that it makes so great a part of our short life useless and unserviceable, that we have not time enough to get the perfection of a single manufacture, but ten or twelve generations of the world must go to the making up of one wise man, or one excellent art: and in the succession of those ages there happen so many changes and interruptions, so many wars and violences, that seven years' fighting sets a whole kingdom back in learning and virtue, to which they were creeping, it may be, a whole age.

And thus also we do evil to our posterity, as Adam did to his, and Cham did to his, and Eli to his, and all they to theirs who by sins caused God to shorten the life and multiply the evils of mankind: and for this reason it is the world grows worse and worse, because so many original sins are multiplied, and so many evils from parents descend upon the succeeding generations of men, that they derive nothing from us but original misery.

But He who restored the law of nature, did also restore us to the condition of nature; which, being violated by the introduction of death, Christ then repaired when He suffered and overcame death for us; that is, He hath taken away the unhappiness of sickness, and the sting of death, and the dishonours of the grave, of dissolution and weakness, of decay and change, and hath turned them into acts of favour, into instances of comfort, into opportunities of virtue; Christ hath now knit them into rosaries and coronets, He hath put them into promises and rewards, He hath made them part of the portion of His elect; they are instruments, and earnests, and securities, and passages, to the greatest perfection of human nature, and the divine promises. So that it is possible for us now to be reconciled to sickness; it came in by sin, and therefore is cured when it is turned into virtue; and although it may have in it the uneasiness of labour, yet it will not be uneasy as sin, or the restlessness of a discomposed conscience: if therefore we can well manage our state of sickness, that we may not fall by pain, as we usually do by pleasure, we need not fear; for no evil shall happen to us.

6 OF THE FIRST TEMPTATION PROPER TO THE STATE OF SICKNESS, IMPATIENCE

Men that are in health are severe exactors of patience at the hands of them that are sick; and they usually judge it not by terms of relation between God and the suffering man, but between him and the friends that stand by the bed-side: it will be therefore necessary that we truly understand to what duties and actions the patience of a sick man ought to extend.

1. Sighs and groans, sorrow and prayers, humble complaints and dolorous expressions, are the sad accents of a sick man's language: for it is not to be expected that a sick man should act a part of patience with a countenance like an orator, or grave like a dramatic person: it were well if all men could bear an exterior decency in their sickness, and regulate their voice, their face, their discourse, and all their circumstances, by the measures and proportions of comeliness, and satisfaction to all the standers by.

But this would better please them than assist him; the sick man would do more good to others than he would receive to himself.

2. Therefore silence and still composures, and not complaining, are no parts of a sick man's duty; they are not necessary parts of patience. We find that David roared for the very disquietness of his sickness, and he lay chattering like a swallow, and his throat was dry with calling for help upon his God. That's the proper voice of sickness: and certain it is that the proper voices of sickness are expressly vocal and petitory in the ears of God, and call for pity in the same accent as the cries and expressions of widows and orphans do for vengeance upon their persecutors, though they say no collect against them. For there is the voice of man, and there is the voice of the disease, and God hears both; and the louder the disease speaks, there is the greater need of mercy and pity, and therefore God will the sooner hear it. Abel's blood had a voice, and cried to God; and humility hath a voice, and cries so loud to God that it pierces the clouds; and so hath every sorrow and every sickness: and when a man cries out, and complains but according to the sorrows of his pain, it cannot be any part of a culpable impatience, but an argument for pity.

3. Some men's senses are so subtile, and their perceptions so quick and full of relish, and their spirits so active, that the same load is double upon them to what it is to another person: and therefore comparing the expressions of the one to the silence of the other, a different judgment cannot be made concerning their patience. Some natures are querulous, and melancholic, and soft, and nice, and tender, and weeping, and expressive; others are sullen, dull, without apprehension, apt to tolerate and carry burdens: and the crucifixion of our blessed Saviour, falling upon a delicate and virgin body of curious temper, and strict, equal composition, was naturally more full of torment than that of the ruder thieves, whose proportions were coarser and uneven.

4. In this case it was no imprudent advice which Cicero gave, "nothing in the world is more amiable than an even temper in our whole life, and in every action; but this evenness cannot be kept, unless every man follows his own nature, without striving to imitate the circumstances of another". And what is so in the

thing itself, ought to be so in our judgments concerning the things: we must not call any one impatient if he be not silent in a fever, as if he were asleep; or as if he were dull, as Herod's son of Athens.

5. Nature in some cases hath made cryings out and exclamations to be an entertainment of the spirit, and an abatement or diversion of the pain. For so did the old champions, when they threw their fatal nets that they might load their enemy with the snares and weights of death; they groaned aloud, and sent forth the anguish of their spirit into the eyes and heart of the man that stood against them: so it is in the endurance of some sharp pains; the complaints and shriekings, the sharp groans and the tender accents, send forth the afflicted spirits, and force a way that they may ease their oppression and their load; that when they have spent some of their sorrows by a sally forth, they may return better able to fortify the heart. Nothing of this is a certain sign, much less an action or part, of impatience; and when our blessed Saviour suffered His last and sharpest pang of sorrow, He cried out with a loud voice, and resolved to die, and did so.

7 A PERORATION

It remains, that we who are alive, should so live, and by the actions of religion attend the coming of the day of the Lord, that we neither be surprised, nor leave our duties imperfect, nor our sins uncancelled, nor our persons unreconciled, nor God unappeased; but that, when we descend to our graves, we may rest in the bosom of the Lord, till the mansions be prepared where we shall sing and feast eternally. Amen.

TE DEUM LAUDAMUS

V

Sermons

1 THE COUNTESS OF CARBERY'S FUNERAL SERMON

I have now done with my text, but yet am to make you another sermon. I have told you the necessity and the state of death, it may be, too largely for such a sad story; I shall therefore now with a better *compendium* teach you how to live, by telling you a plain narrative of a life, which if you imitate, and write after the copy, it will make that death shall not be an evil, but a thing to be desired, and to be reckoned amongst the purchases and advantages of your fortune. When Martha and Mary went to weep over the grave of their brother, Christ met them there, and preached a funeral sermon, discoursing of the resurrection, and applying to the purposes of faith, and confession of Christ, and glorification of God. We have no other, we can have no better precedent to follow: and now that we are come to weep over the grave of our dear sister, this rare personage, we cannot choose but have many virtues to learn, many to imitate, and some to exercise.

1. I chose, not to declare her extraction and genealogy; it was indeed fair and honourable; but having the blessing to be descended from worthy and honoured ancestors, and herself to be adopted and ingraffed into a more noble family; yet she felt such outward appendages to be none of hers, because not of her choice, but the purchase of the virtues of others, which although they did engage her to do noble things, yet they would upbraid all degenerate and less honourable lives than were those which began and increased the honour of the families. She did not love her fortune for making her noble; but thought it would be a dishonour to her if she did not continue a nobleness and excellency of virtue fit to be owned by persons relating to such ancestors. It is fit for us all to honour the nobleness of a family: but it is also fit for them that are noble to despise it, and to establish their honour upon the foundation of doing excellent things, and

suffering in good causes, and despising dishonourable actions, and in communicating good things to others. For this is the rule in nature; those creatures are most honourable which have the greatest power, and do the greatest good: and accordingly myself have been a witness of it, how this excellent lady would by an act of humility and Christian abstraction strip herself of all that fair appendage and exterior honour which decked her person and her fortune, and desired to be owned by nothing but what was her own, that she might only be esteemed honourable according to that which is the honour of a Christian and a wise person.

2. She had a strict and severe education, and it was one of God's graces and favours to her: for being the heiress of a great fortune, and living amongst the throng of persons in the sight of vanities and empty temptations, that is, in that part of the kingdom where greatness is too often expressed in great follies and great vices, God had provided a severe and angry education to chastise the forwardnesses of a young spirit and a fair fortune, that she might for ever be so far distant from a vice, that she might only see it and lothe it, but never taste of it, so much as to be put to her choice whether she be virtuous or no. God, intending to secure this soul to Himself, would not suffer the follies of the world to seize upon her by way of too near a trial or busy temptation.

3. She was married young; and beside her businesses of religion, seemed to be ordained in the providence of God to bring to this honourable family a part of a fair fortune, and to leave behind her a fairer issue, worth ten thousand times her portion: and as if this had been all the public business of her life, when she had so far served God's ends, God in mercy would also serve hers, and take her to an early blessedness.

4. In passing through which line of providence, she had the art to secure her eternal interest, by turning her condition into duty, and expressing her duty in the greatest eminency of a virtuous, prudent, and rare affection, that hath been known in any example. I will not give her so low a testimony, as to say only that she was chaste; she was a person of that severity, modesty,

and close religion, as to that particular, that she was not capable of uncivil temptation; and you might as well have suspected the sun to smell of the poppy that he looks on, as that she could have been a person apt to be sullied by the breath of a foul question.

5. But that which I shall note in her, is that which I would have exemplar to all ladies, and to all women: she had a love so great for her lord, so entirely given up to a dear affection, that she thought the same things, and loved the same loves, and hated according to the same enmities, and breathed in his soul, and lived in his presence, and languished in his absence; and all that she was or did, was only for and to her dearest lord:

> *Si gaudet, si flet, si tacet, hunc loquitur;*
> *Cœnat, propinat, poscit, negat, innuit; unus*
> *Nævius est; –**

And although this was a great enamel to the beauty of her soul, yet it might in some degrees be also a reward to the virtue of her lord: for she would often discourse it to them that conversed with her, that he would improve that interest which he had in her affection to the advantages of God and of religion; and she would delight to say, that he called her to her devotions, he encouraged her good inclinations, he directed her piety, he invited her with good books; and then she loved religion, which she saw was not only pleasing to God, and an act or state of duty, but pleasing to her lord, and an act also of affection and conjugal obedience; and what at first she loved the more forwardly for his sake, in the using of religion, left such relishes upon her spirit, that she found in it amability enough to make her love it for its own. So God usually brings us to Him by instruments of nature and affections, and then incorporates us into His inheritance by the more immediate relishes of heaven, and the secret things of the Spirit. He only was (under God) the light of her eyes, and the cordial of her spirits, and the guide of her actions, and the measure of

---

* Martial, Epigrams I. lxviii: Whether he rejoices, or mourns, or is silent, it is ever Naevia. He eats, he drinks, he asks, he refuses, he gesticulates, Naevia alone is in his thoughts...

her affections, till her affections swelled up into a religion, and then it could go no higher, but was confederate with those other duties which made her dear to God: which rare combination of duty and religion I choose to express in the words of Solomon, "She forsook not the guide of her youth, nor brake the covenant of her God" [Prov. ii. 17].

6. As she was a rare wife, so she was an excellent mother: for in so tender a constitution of spirit as hers was, and in so great a kindness towards her children, there hath seldom been seen a stricter and more curious care of their persons, their deportment, their nature, their disposition, their learning, and their customs: and if ever kindness and care did contest, and make parties in her, yet her care and her severity was ever victorious; and she knew not how to do an ill turn to their severer part, by her more tender and forward kindness. And as her custom was, she turned this also into love to her lord: for she was not only diligent to have them bred nobly and religiously, but also was careful and solicitous that they should be taught to observe all the circumstances and inclinations, the desires and wishes of their father; as thinking that virtue to have no good circumstances, which was not dressed by his copy, and ruled by his lines, and his affections. And her prudence in the managing her children was so singular and rare, that whenever you mean to bless this family, and pray a hearty and a profitable prayer for it, beg of God that the children may have those excellent things which she designed to them, and provided for them in her heart and wishes, that they may live by her purposes, and may grow thither whither she would fain have brought them. All these were great parts of an excellent religion, as they concerned her greatest temporal relations.

7. But if we examine how she demeaned herself towards God, there also you will find her not of a common, but of an exemplar piety. She was a great reader of scripture, confining herself to great portions every day; which she read not to the purposes of vanity and impertinent curiosities, not to seem knowing or to become talking, not to expound and rule; but to teach her all her duty, to instruct her in the knowledge and love of God and of her

neighbours; to make her more humble, and to teach her to despise the world and all its gilded vanities; and that she might entertain passions wholly in design and order to heaven. I have seen a female religion that wholly dwelt upon the face and tongue; that like a wanton and an undressed tree spends all its juice in suckers and irregular branches, in leaves and gum, and after all such goodly outsides you should never eat an apple, or be delighted with the beauties or the perfumes of a hopeful blossom. But the religion of this excellent lady was of another constitution; it took root downward in humility, and brought forth fruit upward in the substantial graces of a Christian, in charity and justice, in chastity and modesty, in fair friendships and sweetness of society. She had not very much of the forms and outsides of godliness, but she was hugely careful for the power of it, for the moral, essential, and useful parts; such which would make her be, not seem to be, religious.

8. She was a very constant person at her prayers, and spent all her time which nature did permit to her choice, in her devotions, and reading and meditating, and the necessary offices of household government; every one of which is an action of religion, some by nature, some by adoption. To these also God gave her a very great love to hear the word of God preached; in which because I had sometimes the honour to minister to her, I can give this certain testimony, that she was a diligent, watchful, and attentive hearer: and to this had so excellent a judgment, that if ever I saw a woman whose judgment was to be revered, it was hers alone: and I have sometimes thought that the eminency of her discerning faculties did reward a pious discourse, and placed it in the regions of honour and usefulness, and gathered it up from the ground, where commonly such homilies are spilt, or scattered in neglect and inconsideration. But her appetite was not soon satisfied with what was useful to her soul: she was also a constant reader of sermons, and seldom missed to read one every day; and that she might be full of instruction and holy principles, she had lately designed to have a large book, in which she purposed to have a stock of religion transcribed in such assistances as she would choose, that she might be "readily furnished

and instructed to every good work". But God prevented that, and hath filled her desires, not out of cisterns and little aqueducts, but hath carried her to the fountain, where she "drinks of the pleasures of the river", and is full of God.

9. She always lived a life of much innocence, free from the violences of great sins: her person, her breeding, her modesty, her honour, her religion, her early marriage, the guide of her soul, and the guide of her youth, were as so many fountains of restraining grace to her, to keep her from the dishonours of a crime. *Bonum est portare jugum ab adolescentia*, "it is good to bear the yoke of the Lord from our youth" [Lam. iii. 27]; and though she did so, being guarded by a mighty providence, and a great favour and grace of God from staining her fair soul with the spots of hell, yet she had strange fears and early cares upon her, but these were not only for herself, but in order to others, to her nearest relatives. For she was so great a lover of this honourable family of which now she was a mother, that she desired to become a channel of great blessings to it unto future ages, and was extremely jealous lest any thing should be done, or lest any thing had been done, though an age or two since, which should entail a curse upon the innocent posterity; and therefore (although I do not know that ever she was tempted with an offer of the crime) yet she did infinitely remove all sacrilege from her thoughts, and delighted to see her estate of a clear and disentangled interest: she would have no mingled rights with it; she would not receive any thing from the church, but religion and a blessing: and she never thought a curse and a sin far enough off, but would desire it to be infinitely distant; and that as to this family God had given much honour and a wise head to govern it, so He would also for ever give many more blessings: and because she knew the sins of parents descend upon children, she endeavoured by justice and religion, by charity and honour to secure that her channel should convey nothing but health, and a fair example and a blessing.

10. And though her accounts to God was made up of nothing but small parcels, little passions, and angry words, and trifling discontents, which are the allays of the piety of the most holy

persons; yet she was early at her repentance; and toward the latter end of her days, grew so fast in religion, as if she had had a revelation of her approaching end, and therefore that she must go a great way in a little time: her discourses more full of religion, her prayers more frequent, her charity increasing, her forgiveness more forward, her friendships more communicative, her passion more under discipline; and so she trimmed her lamp, not thinking her night was so near, but that it might shine also in the day-time, in the temple, and before the altar of incense.

But in this course of hers, there were some circumstances, and some appendages of substance, which were highly remarkable.

1. In all her religion, and in all her actions of relation towards God, she had a strange evenness and untroubled passage, sliding toward her ocean of God and of infinity with a certain and silent motion. So have I seen a river deep and smooth passing with a still foot and a sober face, and paying to the *fiscus*, the great exchequer of the sea, the prince of all the watery bodies, a tribute large and full: and hard by it a little brook skipping and making a noise upon its unequal and neighbour bottom: and after all its talking and bragged motion, it payed to its common audit no more than the revenues of a little cloud, or a contemptible vessel. So have I sometimes compared the issues of her religion to the solemnities and famed outsides of another's piety; it dwelt upon her spirit, and was incorporated with the periodical work of every day; she did not believe that religion was intended to minister to fame and reputation, but to pardon of sins, to the pleasure of God, and the salvation of souls. For religion is like the breath of heaven; if it goes abroad into the open air, it scatters and dissolves like camphire: but if it enters into a secret hollowness, into a close conveyance, it is strong and mighty, and comes forth with vigour and great effect at the other end, at the other side of this life, in the days of death and judgment.

2. The other appendage of her religion, which also was a great ornament to all the parts of her life, was a rare modesty and humility of spirit, a confident despising and undervaluing of herself. For though she had the greatest judgment, and the greatest

experience of things and persons that I ever yet knew in a person of her youth, and sex, and circumstances; yet as if she knew nothing of it, she had the meanest opinion of herself; and like a fair taper, when she shined to all the room, yet round about her own station she had cast a shadow and a cloud, and she shined to every body but herself. But the perfectness of her prudence and excellent parts could not be hid; and all her humility and arts of concealment, made the virtues more amiable and illustrious. For as pride sullies the beauty of the fairest virtues, and makes our understanding but like the craft and learning of a devil: so humility is the greatest eminency and art of publication in the whole world; and she in all her arts of secrecy and hiding her worthy things, was but "like one that hideth the wind, and covers the ointment of her right hand" [Prov. xxvii. 16].

I know not by what instrument it happened; but when death drew near, before it made any show upon her body, or revealed itself by a natural signification, it was conveyed to her spirit: she had a strange secret persuasion that the bringing this child should be her last scene of life: and we have known, that the soul when she is about to disrobe herself of her upper garment, sometimes speaks rarely,

Magnifica verba mors prope admota excutit;*

sometimes it is prophetical; sometimes God by a superinduced persuasion wrought by instruments or accidents of His own, serves the ends of His own providence and the salvation of the soul. But so it was, that the thought of death dwelt long with her, and grew from the first steps of fancy and fear, to a consent, from thence to a strange credulity and expectation of it; and without the violence of sickness she died, as if she had done it voluntarily, and by design, and for fear her expectation should have been deceived, or that she should seem to have had an unreasonable fear, or apprehension; or rather (as one said of Cato) *sic abiit e vita ut causam moriendi nactam se esse gauderet*, "she died, as if she had been glad of the opportunity".

---

* Seneca, *The Trojan Women*, III. i. 575: (Ulysses) A nearer sight of death can stop proud mouths.

And in this I cannot but adore the providence, and admire the wisdom and infinite mercies of God. For having a tender and soft, a delicate and fine constitution and breeding, she was tender to pain, and apprehensive of it, as a child's shoulder is of a load and burden. *Grave est teneræ cervici jugum*: and in her often discourses of death, which she would renew willingly and frequently, she would tell, that she feared not death, but she feared the sharp pains of death. *Emori nolo, me esse mortuam non curo*; the being dead, and being freed from the troubles and dangers of this world, she hoped would be for her advantage, and therefore that was no part of her fear: but she believing the pangs of death were great, and the use and aids of reason little, had reason to fear lest they should do violence to her spirit and the decency of her resolution. But God, that knew her fears and her jealousy concerning herself, fitted her with a death so easy, so harmless, so painless, that it did not put her patience to a severe trial. It was not (in all appearance) of so much trouble as two fits of a common ague; so careful was God to remonstrate to all that stood in that sad attendance that this soul was dear to Him: and that since she had done so much of her duty towards it, He that began would also finish her redemption, by an act of a rare providence, and a singular mercy. Blessed be that goodness of God, who does so careful actions of mercy for the ease and security of His servants. But this one instance was a great demonstration that the apprehension of death is worse than the pains of death; and that God loves to reprove the unreasonableness of our fears, by the mightiness, and by the arts of His mercy.

She had in her sickness (if I may so call it, or rather in the solemnities and graver preparations towards death) some curious and well-becoming fears, concerning the final state of her soul: but from thence she passed into a *deliquium*, or a kind of trance, and as soon as she came forth of it, as if it had been a vision, or that she had conversed with an angel, and from his hand had received a label or scroll of the book of life, and there seen her name enrolled, she cried out aloud, "Glory be to God on high; now I am sure I shall be saved". Concerning what manner of discoursing we are wholly ignorant what judgment can be made:

but certainly there are strange things in the other world; and so there are in all the immediate preparations to it; and a little glimpse of heaven, a minute's conversing with an angel, any ray of God, any communication extraordinary from the Spirit of comfort, which God gives to His servants in strange and unknown manners, are infinitely far from illusions; and they shall then be understood by us, when we feel them, and when our new and strange needs shall be refreshed by such unusual visitations.

But I must be forced to use summaries and arts of abbreviature in the enumerating those things in which this rare personage was dear to God and to all her relatives.

If we consider her person, she was in the flower of her age,

Jucundum quum ætas florida ver ageret;

of a temperate, plain and natural diet, without curiosity or an intemperate palate; she spent less time in dressing than many servants; her recreations were little and seldom, her prayers often, her reading much: she was of a most noble and charitable soul; a great lover of honourable actions, and as great a despiser of base things; hugely loving to oblige others, and very unwilling to be in arrear to any upon the stock of courtesies and liberality; so free in all acts of favour, that she would not stay to hear herself thanked, as being unwilling that what good went from her to a needful or an obliged person should ever return to her again: she was an excellent friend, and hugely dear to very many, especially to the best and most discerning persons; to all that conversed with her, and could understand her great worth and sweetness: she was of an honourable, a nice, and tender reputation; and of the pleasures of this world, which were laid before her in heaps, she took a very small and inconsiderable share, as not loving to glut herself with vanity, or take her portion of good things here below.

If we look on her as a wife, she was chaste and loving, fruitful and discreet, humble and pleasant, witty and compliant, rich and fair; and wanted nothing to the making her a principal and precedent to the best wives of the world, but a long life, and a full age.

If we remember her as a mother, she was kind and severe,

careful and prudent, very tender, and not at all fond, a greater lover of her children's souls than of their bodies, and one that would value them more by the strict rules of honour and proper worth, than by their religion to herself.

Her servants found her prudent, and fit to govern, and yet open-handed and apt to reward; a just exactor of their duty, and a great rewarder of their diligence.

She was in her house a comfort to her dearest lord, a guide to her children, a rule to her servants, an example to all.

But as she related to God in the offices of religion, she was even and constant, silent and devout, prudent and material; she loved what she now enjoys, and she feared what she never felt, and God did for her what she never did expect: her fears went beyond all her evil; and yet the good which she hath received was, and is, and ever shall be beyond all her hopes.

She lived as we all should live, and she died as I fain would die;

> *Et cum supremos Lachesis pereverit annos,*
> *Non aliter cineres mando jacere meos.**

I pray God I may feel those mercies on my death-bed that she felt, and that I may feel the same effect of my repentance which she feels of the many degrees of her innocence. Such was her death, that she did not die too soon; and her life was so useful and so excellent, that she could not have lived too long. *Nemo parum diu vixit qui virtutis perfectæ perfecto functus est munere.* And as now in the grave it shall not be enquired concerning her, how long she lived, but how well; so to us who live after her, to suffer a longer calamity, it may be some ease to our sorrows, and some guide to our lives, and some security to our conditions, to consider that God hath brought the piety of a young lady to the early rewards of a never ceasing and never dying eternity of glory. And we also, if we live as she did, shall partake of the same glories; not only having the honour of a good name, and a dear and honoured memory, but the glories of these glories, the end of all excellent labours, and all prudent counsels, and all holy

---

* Martial, Epigrams I. lxxxviii: When Lachesis shall have spun to the end of my last hour, I shall ask no other honours for my ashes.

religion, even the salvation of our souls in that day when all the saints, and amongst them this excellent woman, shall be shewn to all the world to have done more, and more excellent things than we know of or can describe. *Mors illos consecrat, quorum exitum et qui timent, laudant,* "death consecrates and makes sacred that person whose excellency was such, that they that are not displeased at the death, cannot dispraise the life"; but they that mourn sadly, think they can never commend sufficiently.

2 THE RIGHTEOUS CAUSE OPPRESSED

He entered into the world with all the circumstances of poverty. He had a star to illustrate His birth; but a stable for His bedchamber, and a manger for His cradle. The angels sang hymns when He was born; but He was cold and cried, uneasy and unprovided. He lived long in the trade of a carpenter; He, by whom God made the world, had in His first years the business of a mean and an ignoble trade. He did good wherever He went; and almost wherever He went, was abused. He deserved heaven for His obedience, but found a cross in His way thither: and if ever any man had reason to expect fair usages from God, and to be dandled in the lap of ease, softness, and a prosperous fortune, He it was only that could deserve that, or any thing that can be good; but after He had chosen to live a life of virtue, of poverty, and labour, He entered into a state of death, whose shame and trouble was great enough to pay for the sins of the whole world. And I shall choose to express this mystery in the words of scripture. He died not by a single or a sudden death, but He was the "Lamb slain from the beginning of the world" [Rev. xiii. 8], for He was massacred in Abel, saith St. Paulinus; He was tossed upon the waves of the sea in the person of Noah; it was He that went out of his country, when Abraham was called from Charran and wandered from his native soil; He was offered up in Isaac, persecuted in Jacob, betrayed in Joseph, blinded in Samson, affronted in Moses, sawed in Esay, cast into the dungeon with

Jeremy: for all these were types of Christ suffering. And then His passion continued even after His resurrection. For it is He that suffers in all His members; it is He that "endures the contradiction of all sinners" [Hebrews xii. 3]; it is He that is "the Lord of life" [Acts iii. 15], and is "crucified again, and put to open shame" [Hebrews vi. 6] in all the sufferings of His servants, and sins of rebels, and defiances of apostates and renegadoes, and violence of tyrants, and injustice of usurpers, and the persecutions of His church. It is He that is stoned in St. Stephen, flayed in the person of St. Bartholomew; He was roasted upon St. Laurence his gridiron, exposed to lions in St. Ignatius, burned in St. Polycarp, frozen in the lake where stood forty martyrs of Cappadocia. *Unigenitus enim Dei ad peragendum mortis suæ sacramentum consummavit omne genus humanarum passionum*, said St. Hilary; "the sacrament of Christ's death is not to be accomplished but by suffering all the sorrows of humanity".

All that Christ came for was, or was mingled with, sufferings: for all those little joys which God sent either to recreate His person or to illustrate His office, were abated or attended with afflictions; God being more careful to establish in Him the covenant of sufferings, than to refresh His sorrows. Presently after the angels had finished their hallelujahs, He was forced to fly to save His life; and the air became full of shrieks of the desolate mothers of Bethlehem for their dying babes. God had no sooner made Him illustrious with a voice from heaven, and the descent of the Holy Ghost upon Him in the waters of baptism, but He was delivered over to be tempted and assaulted by the devil in the wilderness. His transfiguration was a bright ray of glory; but then also He entered into a cloud, and was told a sad story what He was to suffer at Jerusalem. And upon Palm Sunday, when He rode triumphantly into Jerusalem, and was adorned with the acclamations of a King and a God, He wet the palms with His tears, sweeter than the drops of Manna, or the little pearls of heaven, that descended upon mount Hermon; weeping in the midst of this triumph, over obstinate, perishing, and malicious Jerusalem. For this Jesus was like the rainbow, which God set in the clouds as a sacrament to confirm a promise, and establish a grace; He was half made of the glories of the light, and half of the moisture of a cloud; in His best days He was but half triumph and half sorrow: He was sent to tell of His Father's mercies, and that God intended to spare us; but appeared not but in the company or in the retinue of a shower, and of foul weather. But I need not tell that Jesus, beloved of God, was a suffering person: that which concerns this question most is that He made for us a covenant of sufferings: His doctrines were such as expressly and by consequent enjoin and suppose sufferings and a state of affliction; His very promises were sufferings; His beatitudes were sufferings; His rewards, and His arguments to invite men to follow Him, were only taken from sufferings in this life, and the reward of sufferings hereafter.

VI

The Liberty of Prophesying

1 HERESY

The sum of this discourse is this; if we take an estimate of the nature of faith from the dictates and promises evangelical and from the practice apostolical, the nature of faith and its integrity consists in such propositions which make the foundation of hope and charity, that which is sufficient to make us to do honour to Christ, and to obey Him, and to encourage us in both; and this is completed in the apostles' creed. And since contraries are of the same extent, heresy is to be judged by its proportion and analogy to faith, and that is heresy only which is against faith. Now because faith is not only a precept of doctrines but of manners and holy life, whatsoever is either opposite to an article of creed, or teaches ill life, that's heresy; but all those propositions which are extrinsical to these two considerations, be they true or be they false, make not heresy, nor the man a heretic; and therefore however he may be an erring person, yet he is to be used accordingly, pitied and instructed, not condemned or excommunicated; and this is a result of the first ground, the consideration of the nature of FAITH and HERESY.

2 WHETHER IT BE LAWFUL FOR A PRINCE TO GIVE TOLERATION TO SEVERAL RELIGIONS

1. For upon these very grounds we may easily give account of that great question whether it be lawful for a prince to give toleration to several religions. For first, it is a great fault that men will call the several sects of Christians by the names of several religions. The religion of JESUS CHRIST is the form of sound doctrine and wholesome words which is set down in scripture indefinitely,

actually conveyed to us by plain places, and separated as for the question of necessary or not necessary by the symbol of the apostles. Those impertinencies which the wantonness and vanity of men hath commenced, which their interests have promoted, which serve not truth so much as their own ends, are far from being distinct religions; for matters of opinion are no parts of the worship of God, nor in order to it but as they promote obedience to His commandments; and when they contribute towards it, are in that proportion as they contribute, parts, and actions, and minute particulars of that religion to whose end they do or pretend to serve. And such are all the sects and all the pretences of Christians, but pieces and minutes of Christianity, if they do serve the great end; as every man for his own sect and interest believes for his share it does.

2. Toleration hath a double sense or purpose: for sometimes by it men understand a public license and exercise of a sect; sometimes it is only an indemnity of the persons privately to convene and to opine as they see cause, and as they mean to answer to God. Both these are very much to the same purpose, unless some persons whom we are bound to satisfy be scandalized, and then the prince is bound to do as he is bound to satisfy. To God it is all one; for abstracting from the offence of persons, which is to be considered just as our obligation is to content the persons, it is all one whether we indulge to them to meet publicly or privately, to do actions of religion concerning which we are not persuaded that they are truly holy. To God it is just one to be in the dark and in the light, the thing is the same, only the circumstance of public and private is different: which cannot be concerned in any thing, nor can it concern any thing, but the matter of scandal and relation to the minds and fantasies of certain persons.

3. So that to tolerate is, not to persecute; and the question whether the prince may tolerate divers persuasions, is no more than whether he may lawfully persecute any man for not being of his opinion. Now in this case he is just so to tolerate diversity of persuasions as he is to tolerate public actions: for no opinion is judicable, nor no person punishable, but for a sin; and if his

opinion, by reason of its managing or its effect, be a sin in itself or becomes a sin to the person, then as he is to do towards other sins, so to that opinion or man so opining. But to believe so or not so when there is no more but mere believing, is not in his power to enjoin, therefore not to punish. And it is not only lawful to tolerate disagreeing persuasions, but the authority of God only is competent to take notice of it, and infallible to determine it, and fit to judge; and therefore no human authority is sufficient to do all those things, which can justify the inflicting temporal punishments upon such as do not conform in their persuasions to a rule or authority, which is not only fallible, but supposed by the disagreeing person to be actually deceived.

4. But I consider that in the toleration of a different opinion, religion is not properly and immediately concerned, so as in any degree to be endangered. For it may be safe in diversity of persuasions; and it is also a part of Christian religion, that the liberty of men's consciences should be preserved in all things where God hath not set a limit and made a restraint; that the soul of man should be free, and acknowledge no master but Jesus Christ; that matters spiritual should not be restrained by punishments corporal; that the same meekness and charity should be preserved in the promotion of Christianity, that gave it foundation and increment and firmness in its first publication; that conclusions should not be more dogmatical than the virtual resolution and efficacy of the premises; and that the persons should not more certainly be condemned than their opinions confuted; and lastly, that the infirmities of men and difficulties of things should be both put in balance, to make abatement in the definitive sentence against men's persons. But then because toleration of opinions is not properly a question of religion, it may be a question of policy: and although a man may be a good Christian though he believe an error not fundamental, and not directly or evidently impious, yet his opinion may accidentally disturb the public peace, through the overactiveness of the persons, and the confidence of their belief, and the opinion of its appendent necessity; and therefore toleration of differing persuasions in these cases is to be considered upon political grounds, and is just so to be admitted or

denied as the opinions or toleration of them may consist with the public and necessary ends of government. Only this; as Christian princes must look to the interest of their government, so especially must they consider the interests of Christianity, and not call every redargution or modest discovery of an established error by the name of disturbance of the peace. For it is very likely that the peevishness and impatience of contradiction in the governors may break the peace. Let them remember but the gentleness of Christianity, the liberty of consciences which ought to be preserved, and let them do justice to the persons whoever they are that are peevish, provided no man's person be overborne with prejudice. For if it be necessary for all men to subscribe to the present established religion, by the same reason at another time a man may be bound to subscribe to the contradictory, and so to all religions in the world. And they only who by their too much confidence entitle God to all their fancies, and make them to be questions of religion, and evidences for heaven or consignations to hell, they only think this doctrine unreasonable, and they are the men that first disturb the church's peace, and then think there is no appeasing the tumult but by getting the victory. But they that consider things wisely, understand that since salvation and damnation depend not upon impertinences, and yet that public peace and tranquillity may, the prince is in this case to seek how to secure government, and the issues and intentions of that, while there is in these cases directly no insecurity to religion unless by the accidental uncharitableness of them that dispute: which uncharitableness is also much prevented when the public peace is secured, and no person is on either side engaged upon revenge, or troubled with disgrace, or vexed with punishments by any decretory sentence against him. It was the saying of a wise statesman, I mean Thuanus, *Hæretici qui pace data factionibus scinduntur, persecutione uniuntur contra rempublicam.* If you persecute heretics or discrepants, they unite themselves as to a common defence; if you permit them, they divide themselves upon private interests, and the rather if this interest was an ingredient of the opinion.

5. The sum is this: it concerns the duty of a prince, because

it concerns the honour of God, that all vices and every part of ill life be discountenanced and restrained; and therefore in relation to that, opinions are to be dealt with. For the understanding being to direct the will, and opinions to guide our practices, they are considerable only as they teach impiety and vice, as they either dishonour God or disobey Him. Now all such doctrines are to be condemned: but for the persons preaching such doctrines, if they neither justify nor approve the pretended consequences which are certainly impious, they are to be separated from that consideration; but if they know such consequences and allow them, or if they do not stay till the doctrines produce impiety, but take sin beforehand, and manage them impiously in any sense, or if either themselves or their doctrine do really, and without colour or feigned pretext, disturb the public peace and just interests; they are not to be suffered. In all other cases it is not only lawful to permit them, but it is also necessary that princes and all in authority should not persecute discrepant opinions. And in such cases wherein persons not otherwise incompetent are bound to reprove an error (as they are in many) in all these if the prince makes restraint, he hinders men from doing their duty, and from obeying the laws of Jesus Christ.